S0-AKP-051

Writing Novels That Sell

by Jack M. Bickham

A Fireside Book

Published by Simon & Schuster Inc.

New York / London / Toronto / Sydney / Tokyo

Fireside
Simon & Schuster Building
Rockefeller Center
1230 Avenue of the Americas
New York, New York 10020

Copyright © 1989 by Jack M. Bickham

SIMON AND SCHUSTER, FIRESIDE and colophons are
registered trademarks of Simon & Schuster Inc.

Designed by Chris Welch
Manufactured in the United States of America

1 3 5 7 9 10 8 6 4 2
1 3 5 7 9 10 8 6 4 2 Pbk.

Library of Congress Cataloging in Publication Data

Bickham, Jack M.
Writing novels that sell / by Jack M. Bickham.
p. cm.
"A Fireside book."
Bibliography: p.
Includes index.
1. Fiction—Authorship. I. Title.
PN3365.B5   1989   89-35368
808.3—dc20   CIP

ISBN 0-671-68881-2
ISBN 0-671-68393-4   Pbk.

This book is dedicated to my teacher of many years ago, Dwight V. Swain, and to all my students over the years whose questions and problems kept sending me back to the pedagogical drawing board.

Contents

Foreword

There are no easy solutions to the problems of storytelling, and no shortcuts to learning the craft. Becoming a storyteller —especially a novelist—is not easy.

The best I can promise is to tell you what has worked for me, has worked for most of the professional writers I have known, and seems to have worked for many writing students with whom I've worked at the University of Oklahoma during a twenty-year period.

If I had had a book like this when I was starting out, I think it might have saved me five years in getting published. As it was, I pretty much wasted my first five apprentice years of hard, discouraging work before I found my teacher, Dwight V. Swain, and began *to learn how to learn* the writer's craft.

Perhaps, however, if I had had a book like this at the start, I wouldn't have been ready to listen, or understand all the concepts, anyway. I hope you will be.

This book, in other words, can only help you to the degree you are already aware of your problems as a writer, and *know what you need to know.* It represents a learner's permit. As you grow over the years, I hope you can return here often, and perhaps see some concept that earlier eluded you because you weren't quite ready to see the significance of what was being suggested.

Beyond that, there can be no promises. There are no profound new thoughts in any of what follows. Some of it is classic drama theory, and some of it has been suggested by other writers on writing in books that go back many years. About the most that can be claimed for this book is that it attempts a new synthesis, and perhaps some new views into what Herman Wouk once called "the discipline of the narrative."

I will not attempt to cover every minute aspect of the writing craft. Frequently I'll tell you where to find more information on a point if you want to look for it. I'll describe a technique, suggest ways to learn more about it and practice it, and move on. Often, how much you get will depend on how much effort you give.

Also, if you are looking for impressive, abstract language, you're going to be deeply disappointed. In my experience, stuff about writing that sounds complicated and deep is invariably produced by amateur critics, self-important esthetes and English teachers out to impress their graduate students. We shall (as they say) eschew highfalutin talk about imagery, metaphor and symbolism, and not even try to impress the English department.

So if what you're looking for is heavy stuff you can use in conversation to mask your deep-seated inferiority complexes, forget it.

Forget it, too, if you imagine that a book about writing should contain considerable content about the act of stringing out words. I think it was George Orwell who said it should be the goal of a good writer to make his style so transparent that he, the author, is never noticed while the story is being read. Good writing is a transparent pane through which the reader experiences the story. Any time a fiction writer commits to paper a sentence or paragraph destined to make the reader gasp with delight, then that writer has failed as a stylist.

Good writers, in other words, don't create "beautiful prose." If it comes, it comes. But it is never an end in itself. Simplicity!

But please also note that this does not mean you should "write down" to your reader. As a sign common to newsrooms wisely suggests: *"Don't write down to your readers; the ones dumber than you can't read."*

There will be little more said in this book about style except to note that I do assume you have your writer's toolbox in order. If you think you may be a little weak on subject-predicate agreement, or tend to decorate your pages with faulty parallelisms and misplaced modifiers—or if you don't know what the hell these terms mean, exactly—then you are wasting your time starting this book. The day is long since past when you could write ungrammatical, clunky copy and hope to find a publisher. For one thing, there aren't enough editors in most financially strapped publishing houses with time to edit your copy for basic grammar and syntax. But even if there were, bad writing tends to make editors so mad they'll return your manuscript instantly, no matter how great you may think your ideas are.

So, if you do have any doubts about your basic writing skills, find a good grammar book and fix yourself up. Do it *now*. Get a tutor or take a class, if you can find somebody in your school system who is teaching basic language skills. Do whatever you must. But do it. Reading and studying a book about fiction strategy when your grammar is weak is a little like trying to study the theory of radar when you don't know a resistor from a capacitor.

One more item: it is possible to believe you are bringing all the right attitudes to the learning process, but to have a fatal tendency to *focus on the wrong things*. It's up to you to examine yourself not only for bias and the arrogant habit of dismissing ideas that don't conform to your predispositions, but also for some kind of ingrained tendency to look at the wrong point.

Let me give you an example. Once I had a young woman in my novel-writing class who always managed to look at the wrong point. One day I passed out an excerpt from one of my own early books, a humorous western novel. Lectures had been on scene structure, dialogue-linking devices, character exaggeration, and plotting for humor. The excerpt was to be marked up for these techniques. When the markup had been done by each student, I asked for questions. Her question (first one asked, of course) was, "Don't you ever worry that what you're writing is corny?"

In addition to being bad student strategy, it had absolutely nothing to do with anything we were talking about.

On another occasion the students were to read and analyze a scene (from a novel by John D. MacDonald) in a study of ways to tell about offstage events while staying in the first-person narration. After this exercise, the same young woman was again the first to have her hand up. This time she piped up with, "It says right at the start here that Travis can usually guess what's going to happen next. Then he gets surprised. Isn't that bad writing?"

Look at what's said here, not at what your assumptions might lead you to believe is important.

Now just a few words about how to use this book:

You may, of course, dip in wherever you wish. But the material is arranged in its present order for reasons. The section on scene structure, for example, is located following discussions of such matters as viewpoint and stimulus-response behavior. That's because you aren't likely to understand the terms used in the section on scene unless you've already digested the earlier matter. So I recommend that you start at the front and work through.

Here and there you'll find suggested assignments and exercises. You can, of course, speed-read past these. You're free to waste your money any way you wish. My suggestion is that you pause when it's suggested that you pause, and do an exercise when you're asked, *and without reading further before doing so.* If you read the assignment, then fail to do it and instead skip to the discussion you're supposed to read only after doing the assignment, you're not going to get the planned benefit out of the work you were asked to do. Again, the assignments are classroom-tested, but you won't learn much from them if you refuse to do as asked.

You will need a set of colored pencils for marking up some exercises.

If you don't already have a work journal, you should start one now and keep up with it during your course of study in this book. As you learn a point or draw a conclusion, you should note it in the journal. *This is vitally important and cannot be overemphasized.*

After each chapter or exercise—if not more frequently— you should force yourself to log several positive work tips or conclusions which you can apply to your own future fiction.

Finally, just one more observation before we start: Over the past two decades, perhaps 20 percent of my students have gone on to become professional writers. Of those remaining, 50 percent thought they were a lot smarter than I, so they didn't listen, the other 30 percent were quitters.

I hope this is being read by a 20-percenter.

Writing

Novels

That

Sell

....

1

The Professional Attitude

If you have dedication,
and trust in the process,
you can become a professional.
There is no higher accolade for a writer.

You'll find little mention of "talent" in this book. Talent is something people attribute to a successful person after years of hard, hidden, agonizing work have produced outstanding results.

What you will hear about is the professional attitude.

What is that, you ask?

It's what made tennis great Billie Jean King wear out several pair of tennis shoes *every week* when she was young, practicing on the court until after dark every night.

It's what made basketball immortal Bill Russell—already a star—study moves made by other NBA players, then practice them endlessly until they became his own.

It's what made the writing of *Gone with the Wind* require so many years for completion.

Great practitioners in any field make it look easy, so bystanders murmur in awe about talent. What the bystander never sees is the agony of effort, study, and practice that made the final performance appear effortless—the fruits of a professional attitude.

What is that attitude? It's many things and they all interrelate.

▪▪ SERIOUSNESS OF PURPOSE ▪▪

Good professional writing is not a hobby, a time-filler, or a lark. It isn't an easy way to make money in your spare time.

It isn't part-time, strictly speaking, because the professional writer's head is in his work even when his body isn't at the word processor.

The professional knows that in order to succeed she must have regular work hours, a regular workplace, and production quotas she will meet, even if other important tasks don't get done that day.

It's far too easy to kid yourself about your seriousness of purpose. Once I went a few weeks between book projects. When I tried to return to the desk, I found I didn't have time. Days passed. Every day, other vital tasks intervened, making it impossible for me to write.

Scared that I might be through as a writer, I made a list of all the things I needed to do the next day. The list looked something like this:

- Work at newspaper 9 hours
- Mow lawn

- Spend an hour with my kids
- Answer 3 letters
- Wash car
- Watch TV news
- Eat
- Read evening paper
- Help with supper dishes
- Write!

I was dismayed until I got a brilliant idea.
I turned the list upside down.
Got up at 5 A.M., and wrote *first*.
Got right back into the swing of things.

You *will* write if you're a professional. You will set a time, a place and a page quota.

Not, please, a time quota. If you say, "I'm going to sit at the desk two hours a day," that's exactly what you'll do—sit. But if you promise to yourself that you're going to do five pages a day (or ten!), and stick with that decision, then you won't just sit there very long. You'll get productive in self-defense. (Imagine the dialogue within your body: "Hey, imagination! This is the writer's buns. We're dying down here. Send her up some ideas so she can produce those pages and we can get off this damned chair!")

The imagination, after all, can be viewed as just another muscle. All muscles are lazy. They have to be worked regularly and hard in order to function at maximum efficiency and with-out undue pain.

If you allow yourself to sit idle at the processor for a few hours every day, and then delude yourself that you are meeting a professional schedule, your imagination will always fail you. Only when you make it clear to your own imagination that you *will* sit there until the pages are produced, only then will the imagination start producing in order to prevent necrosis of the buns. And the more often you force this kind of work on your imagination, the more readily it will get on with the task.

No professional ever was easy on herself. There are always more excuses.

■ ■ DEDICATION TO THE CRAFT ■ ■

Writing is a craft with learned skills. Nothing very mysterious about it. You must, to be professional, respect craftsmanship and give up mystical baloney about "inspiration" and other stuff that doesn't exist except in the fevered imagination of English teachers.

To be professional, you must not only respect craftsmanship, but work all your life to identify and learn more of the skills involved in this craft of ours. It doesn't matter how tired you get, or how discouraged. If you aren't selling yet, it's because you haven't learned enough technique. You have to be dedicated to keep going, and have faith.

Oh, and by the way, you have to be humble, willing to learn.

■ ■ OPENNESS TO NEW IDEAS ■ ■
AND EXPERIENCES

New ideas are scary. So are new experiences. We usually don't have a program for dealing with either. But if we're going to learn, we have to be open to both.

It's a lot easier to cling to preconceptions. New ideas and experiences tend to shake us up. But unless you are already selling your copy, *being shaken up is exactly what you need if you are to learn.*

It doesn't matter where you got your present preconceptions about what makes a story, how you should write, what's good or bad, or anything else. To be a professional, and capable of growth, you have to jettison your biases about what's good and bad in the craft. Even more important, you have to jettison your ideas about what you already know. You don't know —and you aren't as smart as you think—or you wouldn't have to be reading this book.

I have often had the experience, in seminars on writing, of going over some basic techniques in agonizing detail; often I see people in the room yawning and looking impatient, as if to say they already know this, or they think the point is irrelevant to them. Invariably these are the very people who prove on their next assignment that they didn't understand at all what was being said.

Open up!

The same goes for new experiences.

I have a good friend who was once a very successful writer. She decided she knew it all, and went into her Emily Dickinson configuration, holing up in the country, seeing few people, reading no new fiction, writing the same stuff.

Times changed.

Today, that immensely talented writer is unable to sell her copy. She writes like it's 1970 and she thinks like it's 1970 and she acts like it's 1970.

Do you think she would read current best-sellers to see what's going on? No, she doesn't like new novels, she says. Has she read any? No, she just knows she doesn't like them. Do you think she would go to a dance or attend a religious revival or date a new man or listen to a currently popular song or consider the viewpoint of an up-and-coming politician? No. None of that is any good, she says.

She is spending all her psychic energy fighting a futile back-door action against the only thing in the world that's certain: change. She has been left behind. She no longer knows the world, herself, or the trade.

Creatively, she is dead.

It takes honesty with yourself to see if you're like my friend. Think about it.

■ ■ REJECTION OF VANITY ■ ■ AND PRETENSE

Snobbery and phony intellectualism have no place in a professional's attitudes. Oh, it's comforting, I suppose, to posture, boast, deceive yourself about your own attainments and the supposed inferiority of others, but it's self-defeating.

I've met some so-called writers who strutted about, murmuring about the symbolic representation of unconscious paradigms, or some such, but they're never on the best-seller list. I've met others who figured they were really too smart and sophisticated to study technique; but have never seen them in a publisher's catalogue.

Professional writers are people who work hard and study technique and get on with it. They don't bother themselves with trying to impress phonies.

■ ■ WILLINGNESS TO WORK ■ ■

Well, now the cat is really out of the bag! Writing professionally is *hard work*. It's physically hard, sitting for long hours at that damned machine, and it involves a lot of drudgery. Sometimes you have to make the same mistake a hundred times before you finally see what you're doing wrong. Often, you have to stay on the job while everybody else is at play.

And as you were already warned, you have to give priority to this work. You have to make the effort when you feel well and when you're sick, when you're happy and when you're sad, when you're encouraged and when you're in the pits.

And when you're not writing, you often have to do research.

Research is sometimes fun, but seldom easy. It might involve countless hours in a library, searching for something you never find. It might involve a trip through a muddy field in Missouri, or a freezing night on the side of a mountain in Montana, or a ghastly weekend with a couple of insufferable bores in an office in New York. It takes a physical toll on you. It is *not* play.

■ ■ COMMITMENT TO LONG- ■ ■ SUSTAINED EFFORT

A professional does not discourage easily.

For most writers, years of effort are required before anything gets published. Then more years often have to pass before the product improves and better markets are within reach. Also, one book may take the reader four hours to read, but could have required two years to write. Most novels take more effort than nonwriters ever dream of.

No professional will ever turn back from the long haul of his present project, or the even more discouraging years that may lie ahead. If you're professional, you're in this for the duration. And the duration is the rest of your life.

▪ ▪ TRUST IN PROCESS ▪ ▪

How can a writer face the long haul? By trusting in the process.

Sometimes when I face a writing class or seminar I feel a sense of uncertainty. Where does one start in trying to outline basic writing technique? One could start anywhere, for every technique relates to every other, and starting a seminar means pulling out one thread of this rich fabric, and then another, and another, and hoping that somehow the description of each thread will lead the student finally to make an intuitive leap about the nature of the whole.

In a wonderful book about Zen archery,* the student archer is allowed only to place the arrow on the bow preparatory to drawing the string. This minute bit of preparation is repeated for months, no other step being taken. It is years, in this book, before the archer actually gets to shoot an arrow—and then he is told by the Zen master that he *never* shoots the arrow, but that the arrow shoots itself when it is ready.

Learning to write is like this. You simply can't assimilate everything at once. It may be a long, long time before you know enough to be able to experience a flash of insight and say, "But of course! I see what narrative writing is all about!"

Like the archer, to get there you must trust the process. You must study each technique in isolation, trusting that one day, if you persist long and hard enough, it will all come together for you.

Professionals in any endeavor know this. They don't expect shortcuts and easy answers. They chip away at the truth, knowing hard work will one day be rewarded. And the day

---

Zen in the Art of Archery, by Eugen Herrigel.

your own synthesis takes place, you'll look up and say, "Of course!"

And those who haven't yet paid the price will say, "Oh, for you it's so easy!"

▪▪ RESPECT FOR POPULAR ▪▪ CULTURE

I hesitate to use the term "popular culture" because it has a snobbish ring to it, and the odor of book mold. But if we can trash the pseudointellectual connotations, it's a good term to describe writing, music, dance, and other art forms that are popular with the masses today.

You and I may be dismayed when we see a rock star wreck a guitar onstage or make unmusical noises and call it singing because she has cute legs and a sexy wiggle, or an adenoidal freak seven feet tall earn millions a year for shoving a ball through a hoop. We may see all kinds of things wrong and out of whack in our culture, which often rewards the bizarre and tasteless.

When we sit down to be professional writers, however, we have to fight the inclination to start making excuses for ourselves in the guise of intelligent criticism of popular culture. To sit around and bemoan the tastelessness of American society is a sure recipe for failure.

We live today. We have to sell our copy today. So we have to entertain today.

It may be comforting to sit around and tell ourselves, and others, that popular culture is just too low class for our own wonderfully intelligent and tasteful talent to blossom. But it's a chill comfort, and it won't keep your checkbook warm at night.

It may not be true either. It's only in this century that the distinction between what's good and what's popular began to be drawn by academics and their followers. From Chaucer to Shakespeare to Dickens, tale-tellers have worked in the frame of reference of the common people, and have been popular with them. There is nothing wrong with being popular and widely read. There is nothing wrong with wanting to reach a mass audience and make a buck while doing it. Which would you prefer? To write something that you and five other esthetes think is wonderful, or to write something read and loved by millions? If you opted for the five esthetes, you're reading the wrong book.

Does this mean you should sell out morally and intellectually, and always write what you consider filth or trash? Of course not. Each of us has to make his own decision as to what he will write, how he will write it, and how far he will or won't go to try to draw an audience. I hope, God knows, you have an artistic, creative conscience, and can draw your own line somewhere, where it has meaning for you in terms of personal integrity.

But please don't fall into the trap of saying all popular fiction is junk, and that you are above it. If you think that way, then your tastes and attitude need reeducation and adjustment to reality. If you insist on being elitist, I guarantee that your work will go into the attic and never be read.

Deal with the popular taste that exists. Where can your work fit? Don't—please!—go down the path of sneering at everything on the new lists and bestseller racks as trash.

For that way lies perdition.

■■ COURAGE TO FACE OBSTACLES ■■
AND SETBACKS

A professional knows she will function day after day, month after month, up to her average individual standard of performance. She also knows that everyone's work is uneven to some degree, that markets will change, that luck will change, and that there will be wonderful ups and ghastly downs.

You have to persuade yourself that you'll cope over the long haul.

Writers begin with rejections, they live with rejections, and they die with rejections. Nobody sells everything.

It's hard to work when discouraged: hard to finish a book, hard to find an agent, hard to sell a manuscript, and hard to accept the small advance payment and likely small, unheralded printing, with a sale so small you want to scream.

It's hard to criticize your own work so you can grow, hard to start the next project.

You have to. If you're a pro, you simply accept these things and press on. You can't allow discouragement to devour you.

■ ■ ENDURANCE (PHYSICAL AND ■ ■ SPIRITUAL)

Endurance is closely related to courage. The professional is tough, and develops strength. Writing long hours is back-breaking physical work. You may have to hold multiple jobs, and find the strength to do your real work—your writing— late at night, when you're tired, when you feel sick or when you're discouraged. But that's part of the professional attitude. You'll do it.

■ ■ HOPE ■ ■

Very often it's all someone has to go on. But a professional never loses it.

▪▪ AMBITION ▪▪

I remember once in the early 1970s, after I had spent several years stuck on a plateau in my writing career, my editor at Doubleday, Harold Kuebler, came to Oklahoma for our annual writers' conference in June. The first evening, I drove him back to the motel where he was staying, and we started talking in the car on the way. We talked for hours. Harold did most of the talking. He encouraged me, challenged me, goaded me, praised me—so excited me with renewed ambition that I didn't sleep the rest of the night.

The result, soon after, was that I embarked on the most ambitious book, by far, that I had ever tried, a real breakthrough in my career.

The experience taught me something more about professionalism. You can never allow your ambition to gutter low. You have to cling to your original dream. And you must always have the fire in your belly, driving yourself to work harder and reach higher.

▪▪ PATIENCE ▪▪

The other attribute that you have to have, to curb the pain of your ambition, is patience.

It may take years to learn enough to start working like a professional. Years more to develop a career, and a unique "voice." A single book may take a year or two out of your life and return little in the way of reward. Writing is a slow process. Revising is a slow process. Editorial decision making is a slow process. *Then* you wait a year or more for the book to be published!

Slow down...be patient...take your time...check that research fact again...go on to the next project and stop stewing.... Voices like these in your head are good voices, even if you hate them sometimes.

They're part of the professional approach, too.

■■ HONESTY WITH ONESELF ■■

Every writer has strengths and weaknesses. The pro has learned how to locate her own weaknesses, and work to make them better. She has also learned to recognize her strengths, and capitalize on them.

Suppose you realize one day that your story dialogue is weak. You don't start saying, "Oh, woe is me, I'm no good!" And you certainly don't say, "All right, I'll just decide that the trend toward a lot of dialogue in books today is a bad thing, and I'll write without any dialogue." What you *do* do is find models, study them, practice, keep on criticizing yourself, and make yourself get better.

And if you also one day realize that you're great when dealing with character feelings, then I don't think you just pat yourself on the back. Rather, you look for stories and patterns that will let you get the maximum mileage out of your gift by writing stories in which character feelings are dealt with in depth.

There is, however, another aspect of honesty. And that's in learning to listen to your own inner voices, in not kidding yourself about the kind of books you really enjoy reading, the kinds of feelings you experience in your heart of hearts, and the way you really *are* when all the defenses and pretenses you put up for the world have been taken down.

Know thyself, the Greeks said, and there is no harder precept. But in your lifelong quest for professionalism, you should never lay down this part of your personal quest. The better you get in touch with your feelings, and are honest with yourself about them, the better a writer you can become.

■ ■ COMPASSION ■ ■

For a professional writer, it's a high-priority attribute. Luckily, it's also near the top of the required list for being a successful human being, too.

As a writer of fiction, you'll learn to observe people around you with greater interest and intensity than ever before. After all, those people are grist for your mill. But you should never slip into cold analysis or laboratory observation. These are *people* you're dealing with. Care about them. Feel with them. Get off your high horse and stop judging them all the time.

Have your own values, but stop condemning others.

Put yourself in their place. Imagine their plight. Fight to feel as they do, for a change. Really listen to them.

On this point, it's a proven fact that most of us don't really listen. During most conversations, we're either off somewhere else, mentally, or we're already shutting the other person off after a few words because we're busy starting to formulate our response.

Psychologists often encourage troubled couples to practice really listening. They have the man, say, talk first. When he is finished, the woman is told to feed back to the man exactly what he just said. Amazingly, most people fail this test miserably. What was said is usually not what was heard. When the woman talks first, it's invariably just as bad.

Luckily, it doesn't take a lot of practice to start being a better listener-observer. All you have to do is feed back to the speaker what he/she just said to you. You say, "If I understand you, you're saying..." [and then paraphrase the factual content].

Once you get the hang of it, you'll be a better partner in any situation. You'll also have started to jettison some of those preconceptions and conversational gambits that may have stopped you, all your life, from really observing people around you.

Try it. Professionals do.

■ ■ HARD-HEADED PRACTICALITY ■ ■

Despite the dreams of winning every tournament, taking every prize, becoming wealthy and famous, making history, the professional attitude is always tempered by practicality.

At whatever stage you may be in your career, you must guard against allowing the dream to drive you to overreach yourself. The professional always fights to improve. But she compromises to the extent of seeing realistically what is possible now. One accepts one's limitations and works within them at the same time one studies and practices to improve.

You need to deal with the realities of publishing, too. I've had students who almost had nervous breakdowns because an editor kept a manuscript two months before rendering a verdict. Long delays are normal—two months' waiting time isn't even a long delay. And if you catch yourself saying things like, "I wouldn't accept an offer from a mere paperback publisher," or, "If they offer only $10,000, I would rather just keep the manuscript in my attic," you're living in never-never land, not the real world of publishing.

▪▪ ATTENTION TO CURRENT ▪▪
MODELS

One of the main things wrong with many writing programs in college English departments is that the attention is all paid to classical models—Tolstoy, Conrad, Dickens, the great Americans from the early part of the twentieth century. Of course you can learn immense amounts from studying such writers. But it's possible that most of the past greats might not get their books sold today. The market, and reader tastes, have changed that much.

Given such a reality, the professional writer studies *current* successes. He asks himself why such-and-such a novel was a success, and he never allows cheap subjective judgment or jealousy to enter into his evaluation. *It doesn't really matter whether you happen to like the best-seller at hand or not.* The point is that it is a best-seller. And you don't really want to write cute little failures that end up in the drawer with your hankies and sachet bag, do you?

In paying attention to current models, the professional analyzes for every conceivable technique and angle. This time it may be dialogue. Next time it might be to see all the different ways characters may be introduced. And the next time something else.

Many times in the pages that follow, I'll suggest that you analyze copy to see the technique under discussion in action in current prose. It's easy to read right past such suggestions. That's what an amateur—doomed to remain one—will do.

If you study current models and force yourself to be really alert for technique, you may be surprised sometimes to notice new things about writing fiction that you never suspected before. All any book or course can give you is a learner's permit. Writers really are made by studying about techniques and attitudes, then writing (and often failing), then studying and analyzing—tearing apart, diagramming, coding, marking up—published contemporary copy, and then trying again.

Attention to current models and analysis thereof should be a lifelong pursuit for you.

■■ ACCEPTANCE OF CHANGE ■■

What worked yesterday may not work today. Audiences are changing. Markets change, too. So do values and public perceptions and writing styles. Don't fight it. Be aware of what's going on *today* and tailor your copy accordingly.

■■ DETERMINATION TO GROW ■■

Every professional wants to get better, no matter how good he presently may be. Even when you're working on a project that seems within your present capabilities—while you're being realistic and patient—you may also find yourself working on other projects designed to test new techniques and stretch you as an artist. Good.

Don't forget to be open to new experiences. They'll stretch you, too. Travel, for example, seldom fails to fire up a writer.

■■ WILLINGNESS TO RISK ■■

There are two kinds of risks for a writer: trying new techniques and fields of writing, and revealing oneself. The first has been covered. The second may be harder.

Whatever you may write, in some small way it is going to reveal the kind of person you are, the state of your feelings, and what you believe. That's inevitable. So self-revelation should not frighten you, and it doesn't scare the professional; she accepts it, and dares to walk close to the abyss of sentimentality or other emotional excess. Feelings are the nucleus of good fiction. You must deal with them—in yourself and in your copy.

That's one of the reasons writing fiction is so tiring, and it's something nonwriters never quite understand. Writing a strong, emotional scene is a harrowing, exhausting experience. But it's something you can't dodge if you want to excel.

■■ REFUSAL TO MAKE EXCUSES ■■

A long time ago, the Washington Redskins played in a National Football League title game. On one of the first plays, Sammy Baugh, the great passer for the Redskins, threw a long bomb intended for a wide receiver—who dropped the ball in the open.

The other team went on to destroy the Redskins by a score of something like 73–0.

Asked after the game if the outcome might have been different if his first pass had been caught for a touchdown, Slingin' Sammy responded, "Yes. It would have been 73–7."

That's a nice professional attitude. No excuses, no blaming of luck or trends or somebody else's stupidity. No pretending that the game was below his talents, or that he didn't really want it anyway.

Real pros don't waste energy—or short-circuit their own

efforts—by complaining, making excuses, or otherwise avoiding reality. The reality is that you'll sell if you're good enough. Pretending otherwise is baloney.

■■ VERBAL EXCELLENCE ■■

Find it strange that we would list verbal writing skills so far down in a list of what makes a professional writer? You shouldn't be, if you read the Foreword. I simply assume that you can write good, clean, grammatical copy. Verbal felicity is basic in the writer's toolbox. It's a given. If you have trouble with faulty parallelisms, or dangling participles, or comma splices, or anything else of that nature—or if you don't know what the hell such things are—you are probably wasting your time trying to be a professional writer. That kind of ability is where you start.

Your style should be clean, transparent, invisible, a pane through which the reader experiences the story.

■■ UNQUENCHABLE ■■ PERFECTIONISM

Don't ever tell yourself that your copy, your story, or (above all) your effort are good enough. For that way lies compromise with the best that you can be, and as a professional you can never be satisfied with less than total effort, preoccupation, persistence, and performance.

Even in the matter of the appearance of your submitted copy you must be a perfectionist. I assume that you know all about professional manuscript requirements, too, and I won't mention that again. (If you don't, there's a wonderful book on the subject.)*

Discouraged? I hope not. The professional attitudes just listed are common to all successful novelists—who are your competition. The world doesn't have contests in commercial publishing, and careers are not built on self-publishing—vanity publication. So if you're going to do this thing, you can't afford less than a completely professional attitude.

Stop now, and make notes in your journal about what being a professional means to you. What in your lifestyle, attitudes or work habits has not been professional? What do you plan to do about it?

Log your conclusions.

And having said that, we can start learning something specific.

Every Page Perfect by Mary Lynn and Georgia McKinney.

2

Work Habits and the Imagination

*A regular place and a regular time
for work are wonderful.
More important than either
is a determination to meet
a daily production quota—
no matter what.*

Occasionally someone asks if writing freelance articles or work-ing full time for a newspaper or advertising agency is harmful to writing fiction. The answer is that no such other activity will hurt you if you have enough determination and stamina to do your *real* work regularly. Further, the work discipline learned in a profession such as journalism may even help.

The reason newspaper work, for example, may help is that journalists learn to create on the typewriter or word processor, to write on a moment's notice (not waiting for inspiration) and to work almost anywhere. They're all important things to learn.

Everyone is different. If you find that you have to write things out in longhand before revising on a keyboard, there's nothing wrong with that. But chances are good that you may be tricking yourself into taking an extra step in the process of getting final copy ready to show an editor, in effect "warming up your motor" with the longhand version and being too easy on yourself until later.

Most professionals teach themselves to compose on the keyboard. With the advent of computers, later revision then means having copy already on the disk, which you can fix, rather than having to keyboard it in all over again—a valuable timesaver. It also means that the imagination knows somehow from the first keystroke that this is serious business. So it's well to teach yourself to compose at the keyboard.

How do you learn to do that? You start doing it. The more you do it, the relatively easier it gets.

As to writing on a moment's notice, there's no reason why anyone has to sit around, worry, agonize, and manage only a page or two of copy per day. I've never known a writer with such a low production level who didn't spend most of her time staring into space when she was supposed to be putting words on paper. Journalistic work, with pressing deadlines, forces you to write now. But if you don't have a newsroom or agency to work in, you can force your own imagination to produce on demand simply by doing it.

Wherever you plan to write, and whenever, the important thing is to make sure you have a quota of words or pages that you will produce at each sitting before you allow yourself to get up and do something more pleasant. As we said earlier in this book, if you sit down at your machine with the idea of spending three hours, that's just what you'll do—spend three hours. And since the imagination is a lazy muscle, most of the three hours will be spent staring, worrying, thinking about other things, and being frightened and frustrated.

If you sit down knowing you are going to stay right there until you've produced five pages, say, then you'll quickly begin to learn to produce pages on demand, without a lot of waiting for inspiration and wasteful daydreaming. As I write these words, my back hurts and I want to go smoke my pipe. But I am not budging until another five pages have been put into the machine.

The result? I'm typing like hell, and my imagination is cooperating, sending up ideas fast. It wants out of this damned chair, too.

It helps a lot of writers, they say, to have a regular, sacrosanct place for the task. If you can have a dedicated workplace, great. But if you don't, having a production quota is more important.

The first job of any writer, especially the novelist, is the production of pages. Almost *any* pages are better than no pages. Once you have some copy in the box, you can fix it later. If you're sitting around, waiting for inspiration to strike, you're not producing anything but frustration for yourself.

The more you get into the groove of regular production, three or five or ten pages a day, at least five days a week, the easier you'll find it is to produce. That's not only because you'll be developing the habit of writing. It's also because nothing feeds work like previous work.

Momentum. That's part of it.

Another facet, however, that may be more important is the fact that the imagination and the unconscious mind will concentrate on an ongoing creative project even when you're unaware of it, once that project is rolling. Simply being at work facilitates the work.

A friend once told this story:

> I was halfway through a long novel project, and was having hell with one of the major characters. I simply could not figure out what kind of person he was. Then, by necessity, I had to take a short business trip.
>
> On the airplane, I met a man who seemed jovial, easygoing, and a lot of fun to be with. He even helped the cabin attendants serve drinks, and he had everyone in my section of the plane laughing.
>
> As he handed me my drink, however, our eyes happened to meet for a moment. His eyes were like steel bearings.

That instant of eye contact gave me a jolt. It dawned on me that here was a man whose jovial exterior was an act, part of a carefully crafted professional façade designed to put people offguard, possibly so he could take advantage of them.

And in the same instant I knew he had given me the key to my character in the novel. I went home after the trip and made the problem character one of the best I've ever created.

What does the story prove? Simply this: because the writer was preoccupied at some level with the character in his book, the interesting man on the plane immediately became relevant to the writer's creative problem. And so, without having to think about it, the writer was receptive to stimuli that would help him with his solution. Once he had a novel under way, everything became relevant to that novel project. He didn't have to hunt consciously. He had put himself in a frame of mind where the solutions would come.

If the writer had not been working on a book when he took that trip, the moment's eye contact with the other traveler would have slipped away, never to be used.

That's the way it works, once you have a book under way. Everything is relevant. Everything is grist. Ideas come. Connections become apparent. And all because of the preoccupation that comes from steady, disciplined involvement with the project.

There are other reasons why it's so vital to have a project under way, and to be working on it with great regularity and production-quota discipline. One of them is that good novels aren't written; they're rewritten. Few writers can predict what sort of changes may be necessary in a given segment later, after other parts of the story have been written. Characters may change. Plants—a gun placed where a killer can get to it later, for example—may be required. Plot assumptions may go out the window. Timing may be altered.

Why, in this case, should one agonize over every word of a first draft, or stare out the window, awaiting inspiration? It all may change later anyway.

Produce pages! Everything else will follow.

There are two more ways to stimulate the imagination that might be worth mentioning: list making and meditation.

Neither is a substitute for regular, quota-oriented, back-breaking labor. But they may help.

The human brain, as you probably know, is divided into two hemispheres, left and right. The left hemisphere deals with logic, language processing, mathematics, and so forth. The right hemisphere is the seat of feelings, imagination, creativity, intuition. The two hemispheres communicate with each other, but imperfectly.

Thus, writing a novel is an uneasy alliance. The right hemisphere provides the inspiration, the pictures in your mind, the dialogue flow, the all-important feelings, while the left hemisphere provides the story logic, the planning, the analysis, and the words.

All well and good—but what happens when the left hemisphere's logical patterns interfere with what the wonderful right is trying to do? What can you do about it when the left hemisphere starts sternly censoring ideas from the right, when that too logical little voice in your head says, "That's corny," or "That's so dumb"?

One way to get more ideas—from plot topics to character decisions to developmental twists—is to work the right hemisphere (the imagination) so fast that it doesn't have time to listen to the nagging criticisms of the left. You do this by making lists. Speedy lists.

Suppose in your story that Joe just got Mary to accept his proposal of marriage. Now you want Joe to have an unpredictable and interesting reaction to her acceptance. You have thought, carefully and logically, of several possibilities, but none of them really turns you on, and several times your left hemisphere critic has kept you from writing down an idea by saying, even as the idea surfaced, "That dumb!"

So the left critic is fighting the right creator, and you're stuck.

What to do? Make a list. Just as swiftly as you can—and with absolutely no thought as to rationality or corniness or anything of that other bad left hemisphere stuff—write down twenty reactions Joe might have. Fast.

If you are willing to go along with me and try it, make your list before you proceed here. My list follows.

Joe could (I typed as fast as I could, without censorship):

> laugh aloud
> cry
> kill himself
> hug her
> tell his mother
> run away
> change his mind
> call the priest
> quit his job
> punch her in the nose
> buy a new car
> sell his old car
> run to his old girlfriend
> go hide
> change his sex
> change his name
> buy a gun
> throw her out the window
> throw her in the bed
> call the newspaper

Some possibilities on this list are really dumb. But a few aren't so dumb, on reflection, and might give the story an interesting new direction. And at least now you, the author, have a list of possibilities from which to select, instead of a blank page and a blank mind with the left hemisphere critic cackling in the background.

Quick list making in all kinds of creative cracks is such a simple device that many people never try it. It sounds so easy.

But it works, because it stimulates the imagination not merely to send up the easy, lazy, predictable solution to a problem, but other ideas too. And it happens so fast that the left hemisphere critic can't interfere.

Another method of increasing your imaginative power lies in meditative technique. You don't need to make a big issue of this. All you need is a few minutes of quiet time and a comfortable place to sit.

Relax and close your eyes. Imagine a pleasant place—a lakeside or a mountain glen. Imagine the feel of the wind, the look of the white clouds against the vivid blue of the sky, the scent of water and grass and sand, the sigh of the wind in nearby trees, the feel of your body relaxing, letting go. If some more logical thought comes along from your left hemisphere, just watch it drift across your mind and go out again. Relax, enjoy, see, taste, feel, hear, smell things in your quiet place of escape, and drift.

After a little while, when you're ready, slowly open your eyes. When you feel like doing so, stretch and yawn. Come back slowly.

If you do this for as little as ten minutes in the evening, you will find that creative energy is increased. You may see colors more vividly the next day, or notice an enhanced sharpness and vibrancy to music, or make some new mental connection of some kind. You may sleep better, and awaken more refreshed, or uncover new sources of energy. You will notice signs that this simple exercise has rejuvenated your imagination and made it freer and more ready to work for you.

Notice your favorite color in your favorite fantasy. What is it? Stop and write it down, now.

So—

Have a regular place and time to work if you can
Work at least five days a week
Have a production quota

Make lists
And meditate

Much later, I'll give you some other ideas for jogging your imagination.

It's a good idea not to go at anything so hard you lose focus on everything else. My writing lectures are designed, for example, to have the students do exercises to anchor every technique that has been taught. But just as important is the soak time that will allow the new learning to percolate from the left hemisphere, where it's artificial and logical and therefore not really very helpful, into the right, where it does wonderful things.

I can't build in some soak time for you. But I can suggest that you pause and think about your own work habits and imagination, and if you want to come up with magic ways to improve your productivity, make a list. Add it to your journal.

Then relax a while, close your eyes, and think about that favorite color you just noted a few minutes ago.

3

....

The Nature
of Story

*A story
is the formed record
of a character testing
conflict,
told from a point of view.*

Years ago, a famous and popular novelist was asked what kind of a writer he considered himself to be. Herman Wouk, using a term I mentioned earlier, said, "I practice the discipline of the narrative."

The interviewer didn't seem to get it. But every writer of stories—every tale-teller—in the history of the world would have understood the novelist's answer at once.

There was a time when most of us would have understood the assumptions implied in the novelist's reply. But lately— thanks to the artificial distinction made between popular fiction and fiction considered good by academicians and the influx of inexperienced editors into publishing offices—confusion is everywhere. Working editors often have no idea of how "story" works, and depend on erratic subjective reactions to what seems "different." Academicians, who thrive on obscurity they can pretend to explicate, applaud and compound the chaos.

Luckily, professional writers still know what the discipline of the narrative is, and if you're interested in making money as a novelist, you can learn it too.

The epigraph of this chapter is a working definition. I offer it to you as a way of providing an overview of that richly textured narrative fabric mentioned previously. Warning: every word in the definition is loaded, and used in a specialized way.

Let's look.

A story is the formed record . . .

The key here is the word "formed." It implies author control of his material, a formal structure, consciousness of narrative principles, and adherences to classical ideas of dramatic architecture.

Good stories do not just happen. They begin with the establishment of someone confronted by a change threatening to that someone's self-concept; proceed to the formation of a goal essential to that person's happiness in response to the threatening change; provide dramatic events played onstage in the story now in a logical but unanticipated sequence founded in reversal of expectation; build to a climax involving moral dilemma; find resolution in sacrifice, and provide demonstration of theme in an ultimate outcome not easily predicted by the reader, but deeply satisfying in the ending.

William Foster-Harris, one of my predecessors at the University of Oklahoma, said a story and its question could always be stated as an equation identifying the abstract principles at war.* An example:

"religious devotion + sexual love = ?"

The Basic Formulas of Fiction by William Foster-Harris.

I prefer to think of it as the dramatic working out of an external conflict in the plot action which shows and worsens the conflict inside the character.

And others have stated it other ways.

The point, however, is that no serious fiction theoretician suggests that a story is an accident. This is why our definition begins with the demand that the story must be *formed*, and by the author, not chance. Several of the chapters that follow here will relate to formation and control of story, as opposed to the idea that a story sometimes happens by some process of alchemy.

The next part of the definition reads:

> *. . . of a character testing conflict . . .*

and again the words are loaded.

When a professional writer speaks of "character," her use of the word indicates so many assumptions that the mind boggles. For a character in fiction is so many things.

A character, in the first place, is not a real person. Real people when rendered with total fidelity on paper are dull, unconvincing, and vague. A fictional character must, first of all, be a host of *exaggerations*.

Why? Readers are awfully good at some of the tasks we assume of them as devotees of fiction. But one of the hardest things we ask them to do is to take some symbols on a piece of paper, translate these symbols into words, process the words into meanings, and then sort out and react to both the denotation and connotation of those words (not to mention deep processing of secondary associations!). They must then take all this and imagine a person, believe the person exists in a make-believe world, accept the person as real, care about the person, worry about the person, and invest time in finding out what happens to that person—who doesn't really exist anywhere except in the imagination!

Readers understandably need help to do this.

It's as if I were to introduce you to an actual person, but the two of you were separated by a very large pane of smoked glass. I could stand a real individual, in her normal clothing and makeup, on my side of the smoked pane. She would be real in every detail. You, however, trying to see her through the pane, would get only the vaguest, most shadowy and unconvincing perception. You wouldn't see her at all clearly.

What could I do?

In order to make you think you were seeing a real person, I would have to exaggerate her greatly: a bright orange dress and fluorescent red shoes; chalking on her skin; great crimson slashmarks around her mouth; inky covering of her eyebrows and around her nose. And, if she were to talk (since it would be hard for you to hear, too), she would have to shout.

Your impression, seeing her through the glass, would be to perceive what now looked like a normal, credible person. You would say, "Great! What a real person this is!"

When I use the word *character* in defining a story, we have this kind of exaggeration in mind. We also remember that characters combine tags and traits, find definition through self-concept and goal selection, and so on.

We'll talk more about all these things later. The point to be made here, again, is that a character is not a real person, but a contrivance; a character is certainly not an accident based merely on accurate observation and factual transcription.

Further, when I say the word *testing* in my definition, I am aware of what a test is all about. It's a confrontation, a crisis, a genuine trying out, and not just an idle stroll through an accidental afternoon. Tests are active, with give and take, and they have serious implications and detectable results, good or bad.

And what about the word *conflict?*

Many people have trouble with conflict. They spend their lives trying to avoid it. Conflict, for many, is always unpleasant and stressful. "Better to give up or avoid it," you might say.

Not in fiction!

Conflict—the struggle between people over clear, stated goals—is the engine force of fiction. It's what makes "story" work.

Notice, please, the implied definition above. Conflict is a struggle, and in story it's between people with opposing goals. In a story, it plays onstage in the story now.

It is not enough—I hasten to add, since some of you may have already unconsciously come up with a rationalization to let yourself off the hook of facing something as ugly as a fight —it is *not enough* to have the character internally at war with himself. We've already suggested that the external fight should exacerbate an internal struggle. But conflict in my definition means a fight that plays onstage now.

How dramatic will it be if you put your conflict all inside the character and sit her onstage? There she is, your heroine, poor Matilda, sitting on the bench in the spotlight stage center. The audience of thousands is hushed. You, the author, know Matilda is experiencing inner conflict. What does the audience get? Nothing. Matilda just sits there, possibly occasionally twitching or shedding a tear.

The theater audience goes home. "Crummy story," they all agree.

"Wait a minute!" you scream after the empty seats. "There was a lot of neat conflict here! It was just all inside her!"

A critic comes back for his forgotten hat. "Sorry," he tells you. "We couldn't see it."

Get the message? Conflict is a fight at some level, and it takes two onstage now to have it. It doesn't matter how much you dearly love your long, interior monologues or masterfully disguised personal essays about the state of God and the Universe. Readers want conflict! You have to face that, and provide it.

Notice too, please, that conflict is not the same as adversity.

Adversity is bad luck. It's fate. It's blind.

Joe leaves his apartment in the morning. He's late because his clock stopped. He trips going to his car and skins his knee.

The battery in his car has died overnight and he has to take the bus. On the bus he gets mugged. He staggers into his office just as the building catches fire.

Poor Joe.

Right. But a reader needs to feel more than sympathy for a character.

Adversity may build sympathy; it will never build admiration or concern.

And adversity is blind. When Joe heads home tonight, a tree in the park is going to fall on him and break his back, and then by more bad luck his ambulance is going to ram into a bread truck.

Joe can't fight adversity. He has no chance. Adversity will come or go by luck, no matter what Joe does or doesn't do. In a universe of adversity, nothing makes sense, nothing Joe does will make any difference.

But give Joe a goal, and have someone else oppose him. When Joe gets to work he marches into Bigly's office to demand a raise, saying a raise is vital to his happiness. Bigly argues, opposing him, and they struggle.

Now we're getting somewhere! Whatever happens will happen in part *as a result of Joe's own actions*. The story world will begin to make more sense than life often does—be better than life—because here, at least, people get what they get as a result of how they act.

This, in a nutshell, is why fiction is better than life. It makes more sense. It's also why we have fiction. If fiction were really as random as life, we wouldn't like it, wouldn't have it.

That's why conflict beats adversity, six ways from Sunday. And why you must recognize the difference, and use conflict.

What else did we say in the definition of story? Oh, yes:

. . . told from a point of view.

Every story is someone's story.

Each one of us lives in a unique universe. Joe and Arnold

and Sam may live what seem to be identical experiences. But the viewpoint of each—his world and how he experiences it— will be unique, totally different from any other.

This is one reason why fiction must proceed from point of view, which can be defined as a technique by which the story action is experienced by the reader through the eyes (and ears and heart and mind) of a character inside the action, participating in the story.

There are a lot of other reasons why viewpoint is essential to fiction. The reader needs to identify with someone, root for someone, experience the story in the way she experiences her own real life, and believe in the make-believe.

We'll talk about all these things later. Right now, remember, we're doing overview. The primary point is, that point of view means a construct by the author.

Not an accident.

Now we are almost ready to move into specifics. Before we do, however, there is one more aspect of story that must be mentioned to anyone thinking of the novel. And that is the matter of *movement*.

It's possible to write short fiction with very little movement. But in a novel, movement—development of events— is everything. In a novel, not only must there be many more events than you perhaps have dreamed of, but events must have downstream effects; they must cause other events later in the story... affect character feelings and actions... show results.

This is such a basic point that it can hardly be overstressed.

Unfortunately, it also appears so simple—and is so close to the magical center of understanding narrative fiction—that you might work years before you fully appreciate its significance.

Novels may include many, many incidents—little happenings that come and go, and are thought no more about. A shoeshine boy is seen at the curb; horns honk; a storm blows in. And perhaps none of these incidents has a downstream effect.

But if a reader is to be carried along through a long narrative, he must believe that what you're presenting now has genuine significance in the final working out of the novel (else why would he bother to read this page of your book?), that this story world makes sense, and that effects have causes... causes lead to effects.

So—again (and again)—a novel comes out better than life. Scene A is played, and somehow it results in Scene B (or Scene X); Scene B, when it plays, is relevant, and also has downstream effects in the novel. The reader is rushed along, the narrative movement sustaining and heightening his interest (and maybe blurring his realization that you don't write very good description or dialogue!), and the yarn gets played out with a wondrous intensity and an ironic logicality that puts real life in the shade.

Of course very short stories may not demonstrate this aspect of fiction. As a matter of fact, most of us tend to start not writing stories at all, but vignettes.

You know what a vignette is: it's the English department's much-beloved slice of life, a moment in time, strong on mood, probably striking, preciously written.

Here's one:

Night. The waterfront. Out of the fog comes the sound of a lonely foghorn in the bay. There is a street, cobbles, with shabby buildings. The fog makes halos around the streetlights. Puddles glisten blackly. There is an empty bus bench facing across the dreary street to a little diner, where, behind the sweaty glass, are light and laughter.

Enter stage right a little old man in a long raincoat. He shuffles to the window of the cafe, looks in, appears sad. He sighs. Exits stage left. The foghorn sounds.

Wonderful. But nothing has happened. No character, no viewpoint, no conflict, no downstream effects—nothing.

If you want to make it in this business, and if you've been writing stuff like the above, quit!

And don't, please, imagine that you can fix this kind of faulty fictional approach with a couple of tricks. For example, by rewriting the above something like the following:

Night. The waterfront. Out of the fog comes the sound of a lonely foghorn in the bay. There is a street, cobbles, with shabby buildings. The fog makes halos around the streetlights. Puddles glisten blackly. There is an empty bus bench facing across the dreary street to a little diner, where, behind the sweaty glass, are light and laughter.

[Establishing a point of view:] Julie walked to the bench and sat down, tired and lonely. [This is great! Now I have a viewpoint character!]

Enter stage right a little old man in a long raincoat. He shuffles to the window of the cafe, looks in, appears sad. He sighs. [Establishing a goal:] Julie thinks, "I'll go over there and offer that little old man a cup of coffee and make him happier." [Wonderful. A goal.] Julie crosses the street, speaks to the old man. He opens his raincoat and exposes himself to her, and exits stage left. The foghorn sounds. [Oh-oh! Something went wrong here!]

Has the point been made for now? There's more involved in all of this than tricks and paint-by-the-numbers.

There will be more later about downstream effects, cause and effect, and movement, too. Believe me! But for now I hope you may be getting a glimmer of the total fabric. There are many threads yet to be traced.

But remember, story is more than inspiration, more than accident!

4

....

Viewpoint

*All fiction begins
with the technique
we call viewpoint.*

Eons ago, long before the dawn of recorded history, there was a caveman named Hrogthar.

Now, Hrogthar was what is popularly known as a good old boy, but he was a nobody in his cave clan. No one admired him or listened to him, and none of the fair maidens in the clan ever graced his blankets at night.

One day, walking through the jungle, Hrogthar was attacked by a saber-toothed tiger. The tiger was huge and fearsome, and all Hrogthar had for self-defense was his stone axe.

But Hrogthar was strong, and his terror gave him strength. What a battle it was! The tiger scratched Hrogthar's arm. Hrogthar whacked the tiger between the eyes with the axe. The tiger staggered back through the forest and Hrogthar pursued him. Then the tiger turned and counterattacked, and drove Hrogthar to the brink of a great precipice over a river. Hrogthar hit the tiger again. The tiger circled and nearly backed Hrogthar over the precipice. Hrogthar narrowly ducked a feint which would have exposed his breast to those huge tiger fangs. Hrogthar swung his axe—and missed. The tiger leaped. Hrogthar ducked. The tiger flew over his head— and out into the empty space beyond the embankment, plunging a thousand feet to the river below, where it was carried away by the rampaging river.

That night, Hrogthar went back to the cave. Someone around the campfire noticed the scratch on his arm.

"What happened to you?" asked a particularly beautiful young maiden.

"I was walking in the woods today, . . ." Hrogthar began, and he noticed that all voices hushed and all eyes watched him as he told and acted out his tale.

When Hrogthar finally finished his story, everyone applauded. The chief of the clan patted him on the back and gave him a choice mastodon steak to eat. And that night, the lovely maiden shyly slipped into his bedskins, where she was not shy at all.

The next day, Hrogthar thought back to what had happened. Obviously, his telling of a story had gotten him fame and fortune. He wanted more of both. He thought about it.

That afternoon, Hrogthar intentionally cut his hand on a sharp rock. When he went home that night, he told a scarifying story of being attacked by a lion—and how the lion finally fell into quicksand and perished. (Which explained why there was no body for proof.)

Again everyone applauded and admired him, and the chief gave him a wonderful snake fillet for dinner, and late in the night the most beautiful redhead in the tribe slipped into his bed where she, too, proved to be anything but shy and retiring.

"This is great," Hrogthar said to himself. And the next night he told his best story yet, about how he single-handedly bested a hairy mammoth, but of course could not drag the great beast back to the cave.

This time, however, something went wrong. The brave warriors turned away in disbelief that anyone could have so many great adventures. And Hrogthar's bedskins that night were cold.

Hrogthar thought a lot about this, too. "I can't expect them to keep on believing indefinitely that every great exploit happened to me personally," he concluded. And he was very depressed.

Then, however, after many days of thought, he had an inspiration destined to change not only his life, but the world.

That night around the campfire he got everyone's attention and began, "Imagine, if you will, that you are a lone warrior crossing the swamp. You are muddy and tired, and you know fierce animals are all around you, but you know you must press on. . . ."

A silence fell. Everyone listened, willing to imagine they were the hero of the story so they would enjoy it. And when Hrogthar was done, they all felt better about many things, and the warriors applauded, the chief gave Hrogthar first servings of the horsemeat stew, and the most beautiful brunette in the land slipped into the storyteller's bedskins late that night, and told him she loved him.

What Hrogthar had invented was the most fundamental technique of storytelling: placing the reader in the mind and heart of a person at the center of the story's action: a technique that we today call viewpoint.

The reader wants to escape humdrum reality and have an adventure. If you the writer handle viewpoint correctly, the reader will identify with the central figure of the story—imaginatively become that character—and experience the story as she experiences her own life: from a limited field of knowledge and feeling, from one set of eyes, with all the uncertainty—and involvement—of actual experience.

Putting the viewpoint inside a story character's head assures instant reader identification with that character. It's a technique so fundamental and universal that many writers tend to shrug off discussion of it because they think they know all about it. But errors in handling viewpoint are so common, and of so many different types, that more discussion is mandatory.

In fiction today we sometimes see the viewpoint hopping all over the page within the confines of a single chapter or scene within a novel. That generally is not because the writer chose to do it, but because he came to us out of writing for film, where the camera is external to the characters, and consequently he has never had to learn this literary device of telling story from inside a character. Filmmakers don't have viewpoint. They have camera setups. They impose unity on their material through other devices.

With the written word you have to be more careful (than a filmmaker) because believability is harder won in print. When you're watching a movie you believe things because *the images are there on the screen*. But the reader needs help to identify and believe on the printed page. So viewpoint becomes enormously important.

That's why, when students ask me if they can change viewpoint whenever they feel like it inside a scene, I reply, "Yes, you can do that right after you get out of your own single, restricted viewpoint for one instant in real life."

The rule, then, if you want it stated that way, is this: within a given chapter, or (at worst) within a given dramatic confrontation in your book, you *must* maintain the integrity of the viewpoint. That means you stay in the same viewpoint.

Most beginning writers think this is a terrible imposition on their artistic freedom. Better writers gladly accept this seeming limitation as a useful control and focusing device, as well as an aid in building story credibility.

Can you ever change viewpoint? Of course. But you change when you decide to do so, for sound tactical reasons—not because you vaguely feel like it, or have run out of gas in following a certain character.

We'll elaborate on that later. But perhaps we have gotten ahead of ourselves, so let's fall back a few paces.

How do you select the person in your story who will be the point-of-view character? The answer is that you pick the person:

- who will be at the center of the action
- who will have everything at risk
- whose struggle toward a goal is the fuel driving the story
- who will be moved, changed, by the outcome

Some of these observations run counter to the kind of permissiveness that certain scholars would find acceptable. One such old authority* says the viewpoint character can be someone remote from the action and only observing, while adding that the omniscient approach—author as god, being in everyone's head all the time—is a widespread technique.

As we shall see, times change. Omniscience is often confusing, and is generally out of favor in today's fiction. And the idea that the viewpoint can be a neutral observer is simply wrong.

Wellek and Warren† suggest that a better name for viewpoint might be "focus of narration," since the viewpoint character is at the center of things. That definition is bothersome because it doesn't seem quite personal enough. It might be helpful in picking the viewpoint character to remember the *"focus"* word, however, because obviously you can't pick a viewpoint character who will be off at the church while the central struggle takes place at the fairgrounds; your viewpoint person has to have reasons to be in all the right places at the right time.

The viewpoint character should have everything at risk, for

---

* *A Handbook to Literature* by William Flint Thrall and Addison Hibbard.
† *Theory of Literature*, by Rene Wellek and Austin Warren.

reader interest and involvement. *Beware the neutral, observer viewpoint character!* The reader doesn't identify well with such folk, and mechanically such a viewpoint doesn't work for reasons we'll get to in a minute.

Notice the comment that the viewpoint is the one whose goal motivation drives the story. Viewpoint characters *must be active!* What happens in fiction, in a nutshell, is that we pick a person whose whole world is suddenly tilted out of kilter; that person (the viewpoint) struggles to make things right; the struggle is oriented toward a specific long-term goal, and the reader worries about it; the outcome answers the fundamental question that the reader has been worried about—can the viewpoint character fight his way back to happiness?

So, just as a viewpoint can't be neutral about the action, she can't be inactive, either. Fiction viewpoints are achievers, actors, people who do things.

As to the statement that the viewpoint character must be the moved character, fiction analyst Rust Hills pointed out long ago (as others had before him) that the viewpoint character *will become* the moved character, or vice versa, even if the writer begins with a misconception about the matter.*

Hills said that in fiction, something happens to somebody, someone is changed by the action. And that person who is most changed or moved is inevitably the viewpoint character.

Implied in Hills's discussion is the point that you should never even consider trying to write a novel about an observer character as the viewpoint. It's one of those things that sounds good, but never works. Henry James learned this in his first novel, *Roderick Hudson*. James, a consummate craftsman, had hell with this first novel. He tells us in a journal that he finally figured out why. His story, despite its title, wasn't

---

* "Fiction" by Rust Hills.

really about Roderick Hudson at all, but about the changes that took place in Mallett, the observer-viewpoint.

The same can be said about another misnamed novel, *The Great Gatsby*. This novel didn't translate well to film. One of the reasons is that the novel ultimately isn't about Jay Gatsby at all, but about Nick Carraway and what happens to *him* as a result of the action. At the end, Gatsby is dead and Tom and Daisy are going right on with their selfish, useless, little lives. They haven't changed. It is Carraway whose narrator tone changes as he describes the land as it used to be, and who decides at the end to return to the Midwest as a symbol of a purer lifestyle.

It's clear that F. Scott Fitzgerald understood this. A few years ago I had a discussion with Budd Schulberg, a wonderful novelist and onetime associate of Fitzgerald. Schulberg had just finished going over all the drafts of Fitzgerald's *Gatsby*, comparing and analyzing.

One of the things that most struck Schulberg concerned the scene involving Carraway and his thoughts of the Indians and the earlier purity of the land. Up until the last revision, this scene took place very early in the novel, as an introduction to Carraway. Only after long labor did Fitzgerald realize that his story was Carraway's story after all, and Carraway could not have these feelings, be moved in this way, until the climax of the action.

The moved character—the person at the center—*will be* the viewpoint character, and vice versa. Do I seem to repeat myself? I hope so. It's one of the few things in all of life I am absolutely sure about.

But how does one establish viewpoint?

Simply enough. By forcing your imagination to see everything from inside the viewpoint. That is to say, the viewpoint character never sees his own face (unless he's looking in a mirror). And if someone is sneaking up behind him, he certainly can't see that person. And if his expression changes, he can't notice it.

Conversely, the viewpoint cannot know what is going on inside anyone else. The best he can do is guess. Which is the way we do it in real life, incidentally.

The amateur writer of fiction will write "viewpointless" copy, like the following:

Joe stood on the hill. Down below, a crowd was . . .

It was quiet. Then a sound . . .

Something crawled across Joe's hand. . . .

Joe took a drink. It had almond flavoring. . . .

Smoke filled the room. Joe got up . . .

While the professional novelist will automatically cast many such situations into phraseology that will emphasize where the viewpoint lies.

Consider these revisions of the amateur copy:

Looking down the hillside, *Joe could see* . . .

In the dark quiet, *Joe heard* . . .

Joe felt something crawl across his hand . . .

Joe tasted almond flavoring in the drink . . .

Joe smelled smoke and got up . . .

In my classes I use drills—copy analysis work—to prove that good writers constantly reinforce the point of view with constructions like those immediately above. What we find is that the reader will assume for a few paragraphs, perhaps, that the story is still in the last viewpoint established. But readers forget and get disoriented. So viewpoint, once established, must be reinforced continually in this way.

How else do you show viewpoint? By telling things only the viewpoint character could know. Those are:

Sense impressions (as above)
Thoughts
Emotions
Intentions

Consider: if you and I talk, there is no way for you to read my mind. Only I know what I'm thinking. Therefore, when you as a writer tell me directly and precisely what a character is thinking (without dialogue, of course), then you are at the same time establishing that character's viewpoint because *the only way we can know his thoughts is from his point of view.*

Emotions are exactly the same. And so are intentions.

"But hold on!" I hear you say. "I often can look at a person and know exactly what he is feeling!"

Nonsense. What you do, when you behold a woman weeping, is observe the superficial clues and draw a conclusion about emotional state. But you do not know. You can only guess.

And of course you can do the same in fiction. But you can't make your viewpoint God, who really knows.

Consider, for example, a moment where our viewpoint, Joe, comes into a room and finds Anne weeping; then she turns quickly away to hide her face for him. Let's make up two versions.

Amateur version:

Joe walked into the room. Anne was standing on the other side, feeling very sad and crying, and Joe was curious, but when he stared at her she didn't want him to know how sad she really was so she turned away. Joe wondered what this was all about. Anne knew but kept it secret. Joe was confused.

Professional version, with key bits in italics:

Walking into the room, *Joe saw* Anne weeping. *He felt pity* for her and *he wondered* what was wrong. But Anne turned away quickly, and *Joe understood that* she didn't want him to see her tears, *and guessed* she must be trying to spare him. Still *as he stared* at her back, *he felt* confused. . . .

In viewpoint a character can experience his own internal processes, and observe and make guesses about the outside world. No more.

■■ THE TEMPERATURE OF ■■ VIEWPOINT PRESENTATION

Obviously, every writer has his individual style and method of presenting the viewpoint in a story.

In a romance novel, for example, the viewpoint is usually very warm, with many excursions deep into the woman's most intense and personal feelings, long descriptions of how she feels and how she experiences tactile sensations, analysis of her thoughts and intentions, and a style that sometimes is intense, heavily colored by highly connotative words, and so on.

In a spy novel, on the other hand, the viewpoint may be very cool. We may be told very little about what the character is thinking, and virtually nothing about what the character may be feeling. The effect may approach an appearance of objectivity.

How you handle your rendition of viewpoint will depend to some degree on your own tendencies as a writer, but more so, I hope, on the kind of story you are telling, and the dramatic effects you want to achieve. James Bond would never lapse into near-hysterical soul-searching like the heroine of a romance novel. But the girl in the romance would not work as a character if she were super-cool like 007, either.

Whether the viewpoint is hot or cold, warm or cool, will also tend to depend on story circumstances. It's absurd to have your male viewpoint experience intense emotional reactions (which you describe in detail), be aware of every physical sensation with great intensity, and be thinking in an agony of clear perception and uncertainty if he is sitting safe and snug in his warm mountain cabin, toasting his toes before the fire. But if you put the same male character on the side of the mountain, beside a stalled car, with his dying child stuck inside the car during a blizzard—her life depending on his solution to their terrible problem—then that same male viewpoint might very well be presented in tones and depths infinitely warmer than you would have otherwise used.

The more pressing the story circumstances, the warmer the viewpoint will tend to become. That's inevitable. But you may, for reasons of irony or mystery, choose to keep the viewpoint cool even in a time of crisis. That's up to you.

The point is that viewpoint temperature changes. You control it. Know your temperature, and why it is as it is.

The tendency today generally is for the author to imagine the scene from a very hot, totally involved viewpoint. The first draft may even be written this way, because it's always easier to cool a scene down later than it is to warm one up. But most fiction today is presented in its final form from a fairly cool point of view—a moderately detached authorial position.

The general advice, then, would seem to be: *imagine it hot, revise it cool.*

Choose a chapter from a contemporary novel. Go through it and underline in red every word that absolutely defines the viewpoint. Then, with blue, underline all those portions that you assume are in the same viewpoint. If you spot a place where the viewpoint character speculates about another's internal processes, or draws conclusions from the evidence about same, bracket those in green. Put an orange X in the margin every time viewpoint is reinforced with another direct statement such as "She saw." Encircle warm adjectives and adverbs with purple.

Look at what you've done. Can you draw any conclusions?

Force yourself to write down at least *six* conclusions that can be drawn from your analysis. Ask yourself, and answer, such questions as the following:

1. How many ways does this author establish viewpoint (thought, sense impressions, feeling, intention)?
2. How often does this author reinforce the viewpoint?
3. How many different word combinations are used to reinforce viewpoint? List them.
4. Does the writer hit all the senses?
5. Does the writer have her character do more feeling or more thinking? Which? Why?
6. Is this viewpoint warm or cool? Why?

These are only suggestions. The more questions you can think of to ask when you analyze, the more you will learn. Good writers never stop analyzing and learning.

I wish I could face you as you read these words, and give you a shake for emphasis. Analysis is a key part of your learner's permit. If you fail to do some of the analyses and exercises suggested here—or do them half-heartedly, without forcing yourself to think just as hard as you can about them— you're cheating yourself out of growth.

Remember, viewpoint is a vital technique you can never learn too much about.

Consider this aspect, too: your handling of viewpoint is what will make your story, no matter how tired the plot, be fresh and unique.

Why? Because each of us lives in a unique universe. As we'll discuss in more detail in a later chapter, some of our most basic motivations stem from how we view ourselves. We symbolize ourselves to ourselves—and act to preserve our symbol. Our primary motivation isn't self-preservation, but preservation of the symbolic self. We build our lives around an idea of ourself, and we do everything to preserve that self-concept. Even the stimuli we choose to notice are based on our unique idea of self.

If you and I were to take a walk through a shopping mall, we would not experience the same place. You might notice a clothing store, a nice outfit in a window, a candy shop, and the children playing around the interior fountain. I, on the other hand, might notice the electronic gadgets at Radio Shack, the health-food store display, a new pipe at the tobacconist's, and the long legs on that redhead over there.

Further, if you were depressed and I was feeling good, you would experience the mall as rather dusty, loud, and perhaps dreary. I would notice the sunshine coming through the sky-lights, and how it glinted on a girder.

In real life, as in fiction, we reach out to the environment and pluck out, from a million stimuli, those that fit our idea of ourself and our mood. That's why the viewpoint in your fiction will decide *everything* about the story world. Viewpoint is the lens through which everything is seen.

■ ■ A SELF-CHECK ON VIEWPOINT ■ ■

To close this part of our discussion, I want to ask you to check your own handling of viewpoint as well as your tendencies in handling viewpoint.

Read the brief excerpt on the next page.

Then take ten minutes (no more) and write this scene I have given you twice, as directed.

After you have done this work, *and not until then,* turn to the page after the excerpt, where you will be asked some questions to help you analyze your understanding of viewpoint, and your tendencies.

Viewpoint exercise

Situation: A cold and lonely morning, with windy, cloudy gray sky. High cliffs overlooking the stormy sea. A man stands on the cliff-tops, facing the sea, his back to the rocky path and meadow behind and below him. The man wears a heavy blue coat and hat. He appears grim. Behind him, a young woman runs across the wet, icy meadow. She wears only a thin summer dress and light sandals. She is bare-legged and has no coat. She runs up the rocky path. When she is only a step behind the man, he turns to face her.

Your instructions: Write this sequence of events twice—
first, from the man's point of view;
second, from the woman's point of view.
Take no more than ten minutes for each.
Then—and only then—begin the self-analysis.

Self-analysis check—viewpoint

Some questions about the man's viewpoint exercise.

1. Did the man see his grim facial expression? I hope not. He can't see his own face.
2. Did he see the girl coming up behind him? *How?* Impossible! In the man's sequence, the girl cannot be seen until she speaks to him or makes a noise, causing him to turn. (Nobody has eyes in the back of his head.)
3. Did the man feel the cold wind? Sea spray? Did he smell the sea? Feel the wind? I hope he had some of these very strong sense impressions.
4. Did the man have some thought processes going on? Did you by any chance make up an intention for him?

Questions about the woman's viewpoint:

1. Was she cold? Did you say so? Certainly above all else she would experience cold. Did you tell us so?

2. Bare legs. Wet grass in a meadow. Very cold and uncomfortable. Did you mention that?

3. Did you have her thinking anything? Having an intention? Because she is active here, it is important that you give *her* some thought, and an intention. He was just standing, looking grim. But she must have a reason for running out in the cold to find him!

4. Did her sense impressions change any as she neared the top of the cliffs—did she feel more wind, hear the sea, get more cold? I hope so.

5. You didn't make the mistake of telling us what her face looked like, did you? There's no mirror—in her viewpoint she can't see her face!

Incidental question about both excerpts: Did you write the exercises in the first or the third person? You can do either, you know.

Added bonus: To get a handle on your tendencies as a writer of viewpoint, go back through each exercise again. Mark each physical sense impression in red. Mark each thought in blue. Mark each statement of emotion in green. Mark each statement of intention in black.

If you notice one color missing entirely after your markup, or a tremendous predominance of another, it might mean something about your copy generally.

No red would mean an abstract reading experience that the reader probably could never get into imaginatively, and experience vicariously.

No blue would mean a story filled with characters who run around meaninglessly, as far as the reader was concerned, because it's through a viewpoint character's thoughts that we understand what the story is all about.

No green would mean robots, not people—a cold story, and no reader would care.

No black would mean, ultimately, no plot.

Think about what the balance of colors in your viewpoint exercise means. If you realize that your tendency has been to leave something out, then make a note to be aware of this shortcoming in your writing for a while. Practice will alleviate the problem!

And now you're ready for the next chapter.

In two days' time.

Let this one soak.

Think about it.

Mark up a couple of novels, or pages of your own.

Think of the mountains or some other nice place.

Let this soak a while.

Will you do that for me? Thanks!

5

Stimulus and Response

It's so basic,
but so all-important:
for every stimulus,
a response;
for every response,
a stimulus.
It just makes sense!

You happen to meet a friend on the street.

She says, "Hello."

You say, "Hello."

You're heating water for coffee, and burn yourself.

You jerk back from the pain.

The telephone rings.

You answer it.

The doctor taps your knee with his little hammer.

Your leg jerks.

Simple transactions like this happen all the time. They illustrate the basic principle of *stimulus and response*, the mechanism that makes your fiction make sense and move forward in a disciplined line.

Seeing how straightforward the pattern is, one wonders why so much fiction is unpublishable; it may be because it's screwed up in terms of stimulus and response.

Perhaps it's because most of us don't like to believe that humans are really so mechanistic and predictable. The idea of a knee-jerk existence is repulsive to most of us. But money-making writers believe in the principle for ordering their fiction, whether or not they accept the theories of psychologists like B. F. Skinner in real life. Fiction has to be *better than life* in many ways, and this is one of those ways.

The principle is simple, and it's stated at the head of this chapter. When you show a stimulus, you must show a response. When you want a certain response, you have to show a stimulus that will cause it. Following this simple pattern, you will begin to write copy that makes good sense, and steams along like a locomotive.

In our eclectic approach to writing, we won't often mention behavioristic ideas. But for this aspect of work, we need to accept it 100 percent.

Stimulus and response works whether you are trying to get someone to duck his head (you throw something at him!) or plan his next step in a complicated plot. It works in dialogue and dramatic action, and it works in planning the architecture of your book.

The simple transaction is one almost like the knee-jerk reaction. Someone calls your name and you turn your head. Thunder crashes and you jump. "Duck!" someone yells, and you duck. Or—

"Will you marry me, Cindy?" he asked.
"Yes, oh, yes!" Cindy sighed.

So when the response seems straightforward and easily understood, all you have to do as a writer is make sure both the stimulus and response are presented:

- clearly
- in the proper order

- with nothing skipped
- close together, so the relationship is not obscured

Which, believe it or not, some people manage to mess up.
Consider this transaction:

Joe walked up to Archibald.
Archibald ducked violently.

Seeing this, the reader is confused. How does Joe's walking up cause Archibald to duck? It doesn't make sense! But the close juxtaposition of walking up and ducking clearly imply that one caused the other.

"Oh!" says the author when asked about it. "Well, you see, Joe had a gun in his hand and he looked mad.

"I guess," the author adds lamely, "I forgot to put that in."

Right! And assumptions by the author, which she forgets to put in the S&R presentation itself, are a prime cause of confusion and obscurity in such transactions. Stimulus and response provide clarity, logic and movement—but not if you assume things in your head and forget to put them down on the paper.

Putting S&R down in the wrong order is even more common. Consider:

Bob hit the dirt, hearing the explosion.

Anything wrong with that?
Everything!
Why? Because the syntax made the reader discover the response before the stimulus.
So the sentence should be recast:

Hearing the explosion, Bob hit the dirt.

This makes sense.
Now, this may seem absurdly elementary, but in the white heat of composition, some very good writers have been known to forget it. Please don't flip off the warning. Look at your own

copy and make sure you are not leaving out the stimulus, or assuming something the reader can't possibly know from reading your page, or writing in such a style that stimulus hits the reader's consciousness after the response.

You'll find, incidentally, that writing good S&R copy may have a subtle impact on your style. You'll tend to write shorter grammatical units. You will seldom—unless you intend to convey confusion—use constructions like "while," "as he," "at the same time as," because all these connote *simultaneity,* and in good S&R writing that just doesn't happen: you show the cause, then you show the effect.

How about the prescription that *nothing should be skipped?* Again, this goes to the writer imagining something, but failing to put it down on the paper, like this:

Susan collected her mail and went inside her house, screaming and crying.

QUERY TO THE AUTHOR: "Hey, this doesn't make sense."
AUTHOR: "Oh! I forgot to put in there that she opened a letter that told her her mother and father just died." Long pause, then, thoughtfully, "I guess maybe I should have put that in?"

Don't skip! Readers can't provide what you left out in such cases, and the entire stimulus-response pattern is wrecked.

As to undue separation between stimulus and response, imagine, if you will, a wife hurling a frying pan at her husband, and konking him on the noggin. Then the author gives us a long scene between the wife and her mother on the phone, a talk with a lawyer, and a description of the sunset. And then, fifteen pages later, we come to the husband bandaging his head.

Chances are in many such cases that the reader will have forgotten what stimulated the husband to need a bandage, and the whole thing will be very puzzling. Stimulus-response packages need to fit closely.

Check your own copy for simple stimulus-and-response errors!

■■ THE COMPLICATED ■■
TRANSACTION

All stimulus-and-response transactions, you will note, are not as conveniently simple as those we've dealt with so far. What if, for example, we return to the marriage proposal we used earlier and change the response a bit?

"Will you marry me, Cindy?" he asked.
Cindy hit him with her beer bottle.

Or, instead of having someone touch a hot stove and jerk back in reflex, what if we have two men facing each other across a restaurant table, and one of them extends his hand, putting it in the flame of the table candle, and then, instead of jerking back, he leaves his hand in the flame, cooking?

Obviously, something more complicated is happening here!

What we have discovered is that in every transaction, no matter how simple and straightforward, there is always a step between the stimulus and the response, and it takes place inside the mind, heart, and body of the person receiving the stimulus and preparing a response.

That process between S&R we call *internalization*.

In a simple transaction, as we said, the internalization needn't be presented. In the case of "Hello"—"Hello" or the knee jerk, it's machinelike and predictable. But when Cindy hits her suitor with a bottle, or the man feels the candle pain and ignores it, cooking his hand, something more is going on and we as writers have to provide the internalization so the reader will understand the response—and the meaning of the transaction.

Shall I say that again? Okay, fine.

When the S&R transaction is complicated, you may have to play the internalization so the reader will understand the response.

We can fix Cindy this way:

> (Stimulus) "Will you marry me, Cindy?" he asked.
>
> (Internalization) The question shocked her. She had prayed for just such a proposal for two years. But now—on the same day she had accepted Reggie's proposal, it was horrible for Andy finally to ask her. Instant rage flooded through her and
>
> (Response) She hit him with her beer bottle.

Now the transaction makes some kind of sense.

I leave it to you to write an internalization for the man holding his hand in the cafe candle. It might just be that he'll feel the agonizing pain but remember that he must prove to his colleague that he is fanatically tough and self-disciplined, so he fights the pain, fights the impulse to jerk his hand out of the flame, and sits there with his own flesh cooking. (If that sounds far-fetched, you weren't around for Watergate a few years ago, and some of the autobiographies that subsequently came from some of the principals.)

Understanding and acceptance of this principle answers a question often asked by fledgling novelists: When do I go inside the character's head? One part of the answer: When you must, to explain a complicated and unexpected response to a stimulus.

So if you want to drop in a bit about the character's thinking or feeling process, or even a tiny bit of background, you provide a complicated stimulus, and the character is forced to pause an instant and react internally in order to formulate the unexpected response.

There may be times, of course, especially in mystery fiction, when the experienced craftsman will purposely leave out the internalization in order to create a puzzling transaction, in order to heighten reader tension and curiosity. That's a somewhat advanced technique. If you're new to the idea of S&R in fiction, I strongly urge you to handle such transactions very straightforwardly for a while, until you absolutely have it down pat. Only then can you risk tinkering with the norm.

Just remember the general principle: when the transaction is complex, you may have to play the internalization in order for the reader to understand the response.

■■ BACKGROUND MOTIVATION ■■

Please note this well: stimulus is specific and immediate; background is not stimulus.

For example, if Carolyn goes into her medicine cabinet to take two aspirin, and I ask you why she did this, in terms of S&R, *don't*, please, say something like, "Carolyn had had a headache all day." To work well, a stimulus must be *specific* and it must be *immediate*. The fact that Carolyn had had a headache all day is *background information*. The reader, at some mysterious level, will not believe the transaction. It's all well and good to let me know that the headache had persisted all day, but my question as a reader is, "Why didn't she take aspirin earlier? At noon? Five minutes ago? Or why didn't she wait another five minutes? Why right this instant?"

To make it work, you have to show a transaction like this:

Carolyn's headache pulsed, as it had all day. (background)
Thunder blasted loudly outside. (stimulus)
The noise intensified her headache. (internalization)
She got up and went to the bathroom. (response)

In one of my university classes I pass out a sheet listing a number of actions. The task is to provide a stimulus for what's presented, and then provide a response to what's given.

One of them reads like this:

Sam dropped the lighted cigarette into the gasoline.

What would be the immediate stimulus for this?

Not something like, "Sam wanted to blow something up," or "Sam had been angry at the gas station owner for days," or "Sam didn't know fire would ignite gasoline."

All that stuff is background.

Rather, it must be something like the following:

"Drop that cigarette, fool!" or

The cigarette burned Sam's fingers or

A car backfired, scaring Sam badly.

See the point? Immediate and specific and external—not old background motivation that might have caused the action at any old time.

But suppose you have the cigarette already falling toward the puddle of gasoline. What *response* do you put in next?

Before reading another word here, take out a sheet of scratch paper and complete this transaction:

STIMULUS: the cigarette falls into the gasoline.
RESPONSE: (You write it.)
I'll wait.

Done? Fine. Now please don't tell me you wrote something like any of the following:

> The fire trucks came. (This skips steps, right?)
>
> Sam was horrified. (Skip! He hasn't had anything happen to horrify him yet. You have to show the result of the cigarette hitting the gasoline before you can show another response inside Sam. And if you have him realize what he has done, and be horrified as the cigarette falls, fine. But you're just adding another step in the stimulus package and you still have to show the result of the cigarette hitting the gasoline. See discussion below.
>
> The owner raced out of the station. (Skip!)
>
> Oh dear, Sam thought. (Nothing has happened yet. How can he be thinking this?)

No, the response to Sam's dropping of the cigarette into the gasoline almost has to be some variation of an orange flash, or an explosion, or flames sizzling across the tarmac, or something of that nature. Fire trucks may come, Sam may be horrified, and so on. But the *first thing* that happens must follow the cigarette hitting the gasoline.

Also, please notice that Sam's horror—even if it takes place as he realizes what he has done before the cigarette hits the pavement—*cannot be played in that order* because it puts too much between the outside stimulus and the outside response. I mean, the next thing that's going to happen is a hell of a fire. That will be in response to Sam's cigarette, not his horror. So you shouldn't put the horror in because it only confuses the issue.

We'll talk more about the order of presentation in S&R packages when we get into dialogue. For now, perhaps the point has been made.

But there is another point to be made here.

▪ ▪ KEEPING YOUR S&R ▪ ▪
TRANSACTIONS STRAIGHTFORWARD

Many of us have witnessed world-class tennis at some time or other, watching as a great player blasted a forehand, saw the opponent's return going crosscourt, raced over to hit a backhand, sensed his opponent in retreat, and rushed to the net to hit a winning volley.

Great stuff. Pure stimulus and response, possibly with a little internalization-anticipation thrown in.

But even that great player we just watched would have been reduced to utter confusion if, instead of seeing *one* ball come across the net, he had been forced to try to react to *six!*

If it's so simple to see in tennis, shouldn't it be as clear in writing? The rule: one stimulus = one response.

Look at this little bit of action:

Ralph exploded into the room. He threw his wrench at Ted. He yelled, "I'm going to kill you, Ted!" He raced across the room and hit Ted with a haymaker. "Are you going to confess or not?" he screamed.

Now you tell me what Ted's response is going to be.

It's at times like this that writers often lean back from the keyboard and say, "Geez, I'm stuck!"

Why? It's obvious. Too many stimuli. We ganged up on poor Ted and bombarded him with several tennis balls, not giving him time to react to them in turn. So now that we've finally decided to give the poor guy a response, we're as confused as he is, trying to figure out what he'll respond to.

So maybe we make a desperation try like this:

Ted ducked the wrench. "Why do you want to kill me?" he replied. He reeled back from the force of the blow. "Never!"

And of course that doesn't make sense either!

Has the point been made? Have one ball sent over the net. Have it hit back. Hit another ball. Take things logically, one step at a time.

Each time you conclude a stimulus, ordinarily, hit the return key. *Make a new paragraph.* The stimulus goes in one paragraph, the response in the next one.

And if you *must* have Eugene send more than one stimulus at a whack, please remember these points:

1. All parts of one stimulus package go in the same paragraph. When the stimulus ends, the paragraph ends.

2. If more than one stimulus is sent, the responder will always react to the last stimulus sent.

Here's an example.

Suppose Bill feels sorry for something he has done, goes to Ronald, says he's sorry, and offers to shake hands.

You *cannot* write it this way:

"I'm sorry, Ronald," Bill said, holding out his hand. He felt sorry.

Why is this impossible? Because the last thing you've put in the paragraph is internalization, and Ronald cannot conceivably respond to *that.* So if internalization is involved, it cannot go last in the paragraph.

You *can*, however, write it two other ways:

Bill felt sorry. He held out his hand. "I'm sorry, Ronald."
   or
Bill felt sorry. "I'm sorry, Ronald," he said, holding out his hand.

Which will you choose? The answer depends on which stimulus in the package you want Ronald to respond to. If you want Ronald to speak, you put Bill's words last. But if you want Ronald to dash Bill's hand aside, or stare contemptuously at it, you'll put the hand last.

Consider, analyze, and practice your own S&R presentations. Don't assume they're okay, because if you haven't put in a lot of hard work honing your skill in this area, they probably aren't! Carefully take some of your own copy and mark it up, putting stimulus and response markers in the margins, and noting whether you are following the rules. Do you find internalizations? Are they where they should be? Have you inadvertently skipped some steps in a chain of S&R transactions?

Take your time. Don't assume you're perfect in this area. The time you take may make all the difference between clear, dramatic copy and a mess.

After doing some of your analysis, log your results in your journal. Make a note to analyze your own copy again six months from now.

No rush. If you devote a week or two to working on the techniques of S&R, you'll only be spending as much time as we do in a class on the novel at Oklahoma. That's how important we think it is for this method to be drilled in.

6

·················

Goal Motivation and the Story Question

Goal motivation
makes the story go,
and tells us
what to worry about.

Your reader wants to enjoy your story. In order to enjoy the story, she has to know *what to worry about*.

How do you tell her?

You make it perfectly clear that your lead viewpoint character wants something—something specific, identifiable, possibly attainable (against great odds)—that's vital to the viewpoint character's happiness.

You can tell the reader that your lead character wants almost anything, as long as the character defines the goal as vital. The reader will immediately take the goal statement and turn it around into a *story question* and worry about it.

This question is never vague, no more vague than the goal statement can be.

Examples:

You WRITE: Andrea wanted to get a job in the ballet.
THE READER WORRIES: *Will* Andrea get a job in the ballet?
You WRITE: "I've got to get to Akron," Bill said.
THE READER WORRIES: *Can* Bill get to Akron?
You WRITE: Darlene knew it was vital to win the election.
THE READER WORRIES: *Will* Darlene win the election?

Note, please, that these statements of goal are all positive, rather than negative. It's much easier to write about positive goals.

You can, of course, write about negative motivations, like Rex, who wants to prevent Barney from getting the jewels. A lot of great books have been written from such negative motivations. But when you start with your lead character operating in a preventive configuration, it usually means that the antagonist is already into a positive, goal-motivated game plan. And that often means that your lead character has already, in the conception, been shoved into a negative, *reacting*, rather than acting, role. And that's just not good.

Of course, your lead character will encounter many setbacks, disasters and surprises, and will often be forced into a role of reacting in the playing out of the story conflict. It's hard enough to keep her active, and not always just hitting defensive lobs, when you start her out with a positive game plan; when you start her out negatively, she often gets pushed into reeling from pillar to post, trying to stop things, and never gets to initiate much on her own.

As we'll see in a later chapter, the viewpoint character's goal not only fuels the story, but holds every dramatic segment together. Therefore it's vital to state your lead character story goal in positive terms as often as possible. And it's almost always possible.

Good thing. Most of us admire initiators more than reactionaries. The legislator fighting for a new law he authored may be admirable to us even if we aren't crazy about the law. The legislator who is always yelling nay, and staging filibusters, quickly loses our esteem. Maybe it's nearly universal to admire someone trying to get something done rather than someone fighting a rear-guard holding action.

Something else to note. Even though the goal statement given in the examples above are quite broad enough to become the backbone of an entire novel, they are specific. The reader can't worry very pleasurably if your goal statement is something like, "Joe wanted to be happy," or "Marie wanted to do something about her problems."

When I tell classes this sometimes, I detect a murmur of protest from the corner where the English department refugees hang out. I call on one of them, and he invariably says something like, "But in *real life* people often drift along without a specific goal!"

And I reply, "Yes, and thank God we aren't talking about real life here! We're talking about a simulation of life that's better."

At which point sometimes I get another drop slip because there will always be those who can't see that art improves on life, and exists because it does so.

Another item to note: the reader's formulation of the story goal into a story question is always a question that can be answered *yes* or *no*. The story question grows out of a goal statement that says somebody wants something, and the question always is "Will he?" "Can he?" "Does she?" A clear, simple question—and the source of all curiosity and suspense in everything that follows.

In a novel, the lead character's long-term goal thus forms the major story question—the umbrella question that hangs over the entire book. And ultimately the reader reads to get the answer. There will be, as we shall see in the next chapter, many secondary questions, many steps forward and steps back. But the umbrella question remains, and the relevance of everything you put in your novel depends on its relationship back—somehow, even if the remote connection exists only in your viewpoint's mind—to the original goal statement.

Look at nearly any formed novel you ever enjoyed, read with great tension and curiosity and suspense. From virtually the first page you knew what the long-term goal was, and you had your story question. Often it was made perfectly explicit in the text itself. Sometimes you guessed it from the context and hints the author gave you. But you knew what you were worrying about.

Do you want to start your book in a way that makes sense, and will involve the reader? Then establish your lead character and let her tell another character, or allow yourself to speak for her, precisely what she wants, and why it's vital to her. The reader will turn it into a story question, and start reading with interest.

Of course you need more than that to keep the story going. It's all well and good to set up a character and a goal, but if the character gets the goal too soon or too easily, your book dies. The key to maintaining reader tension and interest is to delay the climax *by putting obstacles between the character and attainment of the goal.*

How do you do that? By now I hope you sense the answer. You do it by setting up another character who has a vested interest in reaching the lead's goal before she does, or in thwarting the lead's quest.

In a word: conflict.

Every good novel is, at some level, the record of a quest.

For a quest to have continuing interest, you need not only adversity, but conflict, standing between the lead and the goal.

In a writing career spanning almost forty years, I have had three serious slumps—times when the ideas simply would not come, and everything I wrote felt sour and insipid. On one of those occasions, I sensed that my imagination had grown weary of developing story material. It's hard work. Once I sensed this, I refreshed my imagination by allowing it, for a while, to do just the opposite—writing ideas in which I made no effort to interpose problems between the lead character and attainment of the goal. What came out were all the shortest "novels" in the world:

> He always wanted her and he got her.

That's the end of that "novel." Or,

> She had to escape and she did.

That's the end of that one. Or,

> "Say yes!"
> "Yes!"

Which ends that. Or, one for the English department,

> He was depressed so he killed himself.

Great! Something "downlifting"!

I hope you get the point. Many would-be novelists make the narrative job much harder than it has to be by making things too easy on the hero. *Nothing in storytelling fails like letting the lead character succeed.* So, once the lead character has established a long-term goal, then the reader forms an um-brella story question, and then you provide another character as the source of active conflict to make sure nothing comes easy for the lead, and the reader worries like hell and gets a tum-myache and stays up half the night reading your novel—and loves it.

Of course if you don't want editors, and then readers, stay-ing up half the night with a suspense tummyache reading your novel, do it some other way. As people say, there's more than one way to skin a cat. After you do it another way and don't sell your novel, you may *need* to skin a cat—before you have it for supper.

Look at your own novel. If you were to send it to me in its present form, would I know very early on:

Who the lead character is
What specifically he wants
Why it's vital to his happiness
Who stands between him and attainment?

I hope so.

But, another word of warning. In real life we often confront opposition of a vast and amorphous kind. "Society" seems against us, or the "church," or "Most people don't like that." In fiction, while the opposition may be powerful and widespread, the dramaturgy works infinitely better if the lead character and the major source of opposition are *people*, not organizations or social entities.

A story is the playing out of a moral equation of some kind, and it's much more fun for the reader if she can identify the sides *in individual characters*.

I refer you again to the concept of putting your novel on a stage before a live audience. If your play opens with a huge, blobby, brown *shape* coming out with a sign on its back, "Forces of unselfish good," and then entering stage left comes a long, slinky, creepy *other shape* labeled "Bad guys in sassiety," I don't think the audience is going to stay long.

People identify with people, not abstract concepts.

Same in a novel, okay?

The idea of giving a novel a spine through statement of a long-term goal is so simple that a lot of writers never get it. They want to be subtle. Be subtle at your own risk.

Well, all well and good, you may say. But how do I know how to pick a goal for a lead character? How do I know it's important (big) enough? How do I know the reader won't yawn, or think it's dumb?

In the first place, every writer has a chronic fear of writing something dumb. The fear keeps a lot of writers well back from the edge, writing stuff that's safe or tried-and-true. This kind of fear, common as it is, is deadly. You have to be willing to risk being dumb. Chances are you won't be.

So how do you pick a lead character's goal? To answer that question requires another brief excursion into psychology. But I guarantee it won't be painful.

Fairly early in this century, when Freudians were doing their free association thing and Jung was developing his theory of the collective unconscious and Karen Horney was somewhere in the middle ground, there was another psychologist at work in the northeastern United States whose name never got very well known, but whose basic theory is more useful to a novelist than most of the things done by the others just named.

This man's name was Prescott Leckey, and, according to S. I. Hayakawa,* what Leckey essentially said was this: Every human's most vital task in life is the preservation and enhancement of his concept of himself.

Or, to put it another way, as Hayakawa does in discussing Leckey, the primary goal of a human is not self-preservation, but preservation of the symbolic self.

Why else, Hayakawa asks, would a man spend $300 a year on equipment to catch $2 worth of fish? Or why would a young woman skip lunch for years to buy a fur coat? And, I might add, why would a soldier throw his body on a live grenade to save his comrades, but assuring his own physical obliteration?

We begin very early in life in forming a self-concept. We test it, and if it seems reasonably accurate, we begin to define ourselves more specifically by it. "I'm a man of action." Or, "I'm a lady of quality." Or, "I'm a brilliant writer, but I can't do math." Once we start making such judgments about ourselves, the die is cast. We work to become more of what we are.

So the young woman in the story who tells her boyfriend in

Symbol, Status and Personality by S. I. Hayakawa.

the back seat of his car, "Oh, I can't do that! *I'm not that kind of girl!*" is being more accurate than she realizes. We do things, or refuse to do them, precisely for such reasons.

The self-concept is that view of oneself, positive or negative, that is admissible to consciousness. Scratch a story character (or a person) and she is apt to tell you, "I would never go without a bra because I'm not that kind of person!" (whatever "kind of person" that is) or, "I can't dance; I've always been clumsy and shy." There is nothing mysterious or vague about the self-concept in terms of the unconscious or preconscious. The self-concept is *there*, and people know what they think they are . . . and aren't.

In real life, and in fiction, people generally don't like everything in their concept of themselves, but they've reached accommodations: the shy little girl writes poetry but stays out of school plays; the other little girl who defines herself as socially at ease and extroverted may shun writing poetry, but will jump at any chance to perform. Joe grabs every chance to climb a cliff or ride a cycle or walk a ledge or swim in the quarry. Why does he take such risks? "I'm just that kind of guy," he'll tell you.

Self-concepts can be positive or negative. There's a story of a substitute teacher who went into a classroom of gifted children one week. She found they were outstanding in everything except math. They couldn't do *anything* in math.

Puzzled, the substitute teacher did some detective work and learned that an earlier teacher of this class had said one day in exasperation, "I've never seen a class like this one! *You people just can't do math!*"

The kids had taken the information in, and in a twinkling it became part of their self-concept as a group. They were the class that couldn't do math. So of course they didn't!

The substitute teacher took days, tricking the kids into doing word problems (which, having the self-concept of being good readers, they could of course do), and finally told them, "Hey, these word problems you've been doing are full of math.

So you guys have changed. Now you are the class that can also do math!"

And so the class's self-concept changed, and the problem vanished.

I often encounter students who tell me, with the chuckle of the witch parent, "I just can't spell."

"Up until now you may have thought of yourself as a person who couldn't spell," I reply. "But from this moment forward, you will please remember that you are also the person who knows how to look words up in the dictionary, and will do so, in order to pass."

It works.

So the self-concept, which often lags the person's present reality, is vitally important. We dress, work, play roles, buy cars, pick restaurants and friends, do some things and shun other activities—all because of who and what we think we are. We have a self-definition, and we do everything in our power to protect and enhance it.

All this according to Leckey.

Do you see the relevance to selection of story goal by a character? I hope so. Preservation of the symbolic self is our number one priority. If something will help the character repair a battered self-concept, or enhance an existing one, then that something will be essential to the character's happiness— and he will die to get it.

And so a man spends all his life searching for the identity of his real father, because he is the kind of man who believes he can never feel whole until he knows, because he is not the kind of man who gives up. Or a woman stays with a man who drinks, and beats her, because she is not the kind of woman who divorces. Or a villain begins a murderous round of visits to former jurors who sent him to prison because he is not the kind of man who forgives or forgets. None of these quests has to be logical by any standard outside that dictated by the self-concept of the given character.

The trick in planning problems in a novel—in matching

problem with self-concept with goal—lies in finding either a character for whom your planned problem will create a crisis, or finding a problem that will threaten the self-concept of your planned character. Some writers start with character, some with plot. They all get to the same place.

Suppose, for example, we go back to our two young girls we mentioned earlier, the one who sees herself as a poet who shuns the spotlight, and the other who sees herself as socially easygoing and wonderful.

Now let's assume we want to write a story in which the teacher goes to a child in the class and says, "Millicent, I have wonderful news! You have been picked to sing at the school Christmas party, and do a little dance."

For little girl A, this plot premise is a disaster. After all, *she* is the little girl who can't do things like that. The idea of performing in public makes her sick. It doesn't fit her self-concept. She will immediately pick some plan, some goal, to get herself out of the situation and restore the feeling of balance with her self-concept.

So for little girl A, this is a good plot.

But what about little girl *B?* She thinks of herself as socially adept, remember. Given the same assignment, she sees no circumstance that threatens her self-concept in any way. "Great!" she says gleefully. "I'll bring my tutu. Can I play the harmonica too?" For her, our plot idea doesn't work at all. She doesn't need to pick any new goal. She's happy just as she is.

That's what I mean when I say you start either with a plot, and find a character whose self-concept will be threatened by it, or you pick a character and then build up a plot that will be threatening. Mix and match. As long as you don't write about passive characters (and we've already mentioned that injunction), then the character will form a goal, you will provide opposition, and the story is under way.

During the writing of your novel, incidentally, characters may often further define themselves for the reader by stating—and even arguing about—their self-concept. We'll talk more about that in a later chapter.

Goal motivation, stemming from deeply felt needs for happiness, defines specifically and clearly what the lead character wants. The reader forms a story question from that, and has the suspense-curiosity umbrella that will cover everything, all the twists and turns, in the longest plot, provided the climax is delayed again and again, through conflict.

Now here's an assignment for you.

Look at four or five published novels. Notice how goal comes up early, is repeated often, is confronted constantly by other people with opposing goals—conflict. Underline passages that stress these factors. Analyze how they are stated or introduced and developed, how they are repeated throughout the book. Make notes on different ways *you* can specify goal statement.

Log your conclusions in your journal.

Because this is vital, let me suggest that you give yourself more soak time on the matter, and other aspects discussed in recent chapters, before you press on. You can read a book like this one straight through in an hour or two, and thus be very efficient. The problem will be that you'll only register whatever you already know, and will miss everything that's new to you—the very stuff you bought the book to learn.

How can you avoid this? By taking seriously what sometimes may appear to be casual assignments. They aren't offered casually, and if you want to take in the maximum amount of information, learn the most, you'll pause and do the work. Speed-reading piles up "finished" books in the corner of the living room. It doesn't teach you much. No one is keeping a clock on how fast you finish this book. But the next editor's reaction may tell you. And you want that message to be pleasant, don't you?

Good. Slow down. If you don't want to do the work, just gestate for a few days and think of the color yellow.

7

•••••••••••••••••

How a Story Starts
...and How It Ends

Story begins with change,
and ends in sacrificial
decision and reversal.

In his wonderful book, *The Ordeal of Change,** the late long-shoreman-philosopher Eric Hoffer tells about a time during the great depression of the 1930s when he was a migrant farm worker in the Pacific Northwest. Hoffer and his friends, it seems, were working for an hourly wage, picking a certain kind of vegetable.

One evening the foreman came to the workers and told them to get on the boxcars nearby because they were being taken to California, where they would pick a very similar—but different—vegetable.

Racketing down the West Coast on the train that night,

**The Ordeal of Change* by Eric Hoffer.

Hoffer noticed his companions in all kinds of discomfort. Perhaps they were drinking or fighting or looking morose; Hoffer detected in himself some real fear.

This, he thought, was ridiculous. There simply wasn't much difference between picking, say, green beans and peas. But then he had an insight that helped him understand. We know we can pick green beans, he thought. But we don't know yet if we can pick peas. And so he learned that virtually any change, however seemingly insignificant, is threatening.

From the last chapter we can understand why. We build an environment to support our self-concept. We act within the demands and limitations of that self-concept. If we are thus in harmony with our environment, then all is well and we feel comfortable.

But enter change. *Any change*. The environment is subtly altered. We and our self-concept are no longer in harmony with it. We are uncomfortable—even scared.

The best stories all start with change for this reason. A stranger arrives in town. A new family moves in on the block. A marriage begins or ends. A baby is born. The first leaves of autumn fall. A letter arrives. The telephone rings. Something happens to change things for the viewpoint character, and a story begins.

Notice in your reading of popular novels how very, very often the moment of change is the moment the book begins. Notice, too, how often the seasoned professional will use the word *change* within the first couple of pages of the novel.

Change means lack of harmony with the environment, a threat to the self-concept. Since the self-concept is our most precious possession, we will fight to protect it—to find a new harmony. We will do something. The something we select will be our story goal, and the reader will see the story question in that. And we are off.

Beyond this observation, a few other matters might be addressed briefly on the subject of starting your story.

■ ■ Never Warm Up Your ■ ■ Engines

I've often had the experience of sitting down with a student manuscript and being confronted by a long recitation of story backdrop, or lengthy description of the setting, or analysis of a character before the character gets onstage. When I wake up later and ask the student why he started in such a dull manner, he always says with a frown, "Well, there was all this stuff I had to set up."

All such stuff is warming up of your creative engines. It has no place starting your actual manuscript. They warm up their engines before the start of a motor race, too. But nobody comes to see that.

Most of the things you think you need to set up are author concerns. The reader doesn't give a damn. She wants the story to start.

So start it. If you must, drag in all that background and description later, after your reader has been hooked by the story.

■ ■ Establish a Threat or Worry ■ ■ at Once

Some writers do this by beginning with a prologue or very brief first chapter in which the villain of the piece is introduced and shown doing some dastardly deed before we even meet the hero. Others show something mysterious happening, then switch to the hero. Some give a hook with a topic-sentence promise, as one novelist did when, in effect, he said, "It began like a normal day, and I had no suspicion that by nightfall my life would be wrecked." Or consider the much-loved opener of one of John D. MacDonald's Travis McGee novels:

> We were about to give up and call it a night when somebody dropped the girl off the bridge.*

Beautiful! Just like that.

Your novel may not have such a dramatic start. But you can identify the threat or hook that is inherent in your opening situation, and you can hit the reader with it *at once*.

Remember, your first reader will be the jaded editor. You have perhaps twenty-five words to engage her interest.

■ ■ KEEP CHARACTER CONFUSION ■ ■
TO A MINIMUM

By this I simply mean that readers take time to get to know characters. Your novel may end up with a cast of thousands, but you must introduce them carefully, *one or two at a time*.

If your first scene at the moment has Jack and Bill and Arnold and Linda in conversation at dinner, the reader is going to be swamped, and so will you be, trying to introduce so many people at once, and also establish time and place and threat in the novel.

The solution is to go back and have Jack and Linda be late, and Bill just standing up to greet Arnold as the novel opens.

Darker than Amber by John D. MacDonald.

Then, once they're established (and maybe we know that Bill has a bank foreclosure notice in his pocket that threatens to destroy his life), we can bring in Linda, while Jack checks the coats, and then finally bring Jack into the scene.

One of the commonest causes of early confusion in a book is a big cast ("big" meaning more than three!) introduced too early and too swiftly for reader clarity. Keep your character confusion to a minimum by planning story tactics that avoid mob scenes.

▪▪ GET SOMETHING HAPPENING ▪▪

Set up an early hook, a surprise or twist that will make the reader gasp and turn the pages to find out what happens next.

Finally, no matter how complicated your novel is going to be, keep the opening simple. Remember that your goal on the first page is to get the reader to read the second! Everything else can come later. Simplify, simplify!

As to ending a story, especially a novel, the words we said earlier about fiction dealing with a moral equation are crucial here. The mechanism is as old as storytelling. Perception of the universal chord it strikes in humankind, and analysis of how it works, were best done by my departed colleague at the University of Oklahoma, William Foster-Harris, whose book on the subject *(The Basic Formulas of Fiction)* still stands like a rock in the literature of writing technique.

Let's review and elaborate on what I said earlier about story and the moral equation, as explained by Foster-Harris. At some level, Foster-Harris said, every story deals with an internal, as well as external, struggle. The tension inside the viewpoint character is a war between opposing ideals or loyalties. As the title of his book implies, this struggle can be expressed as an equation:

$$\text{Value } 1 + \text{Value } 2 = \text{unknown outcome}$$

Or, as it could be expressed in more nearly mathematical terms:

$$V1 + V2 = ?$$

Example: A story of struggle might involve an old man who, far past the age for fathering children, had a son whom he loved beyond all else on earth. But the old man, who had spent his long life loving and honoring his God, might be called by the voice of God one day to take his son to the top of a mountain. And, once there, God might have told the old man to sacrifice the son to show love for the God.

In this case (roughly the story of Abraham and Isaac in the Bible), the old man was confronted with the cruelest dilemma: he had to make a choice between love of his God and love of his son.

In Foster-Harris's terms: Parental love versus love for God will end with—? Or:

$$PL + LG = ?$$

It was Foster-Harris's contention that most of the great stories of all time somehow take part in this archetypal pattern of having plot finally devolve to a moment where the central character is forced to the ultimate moral dilemma where no choice looks good and circumstance absolutely forces the character to make a decision in action, now, and based on who and what he ultimately is.

Such a test in the climax of a story (of whatever length) is the final crisis and test of the worth of the character. Surely, if the story has been of a sympathetic character, we as readers want the character to make the good choice. But, as in the case of the Hebrew readers of the story of Abraham, the good decision may appear to be sacrificial—in Abraham's case, literally so.

There is no doubt that to early readers (or hearers) of the Abraham story, the good decision was to sacrifice Isaac. But this was also clearly a sacrifice in more ways than one. Abraham evidently stood to lose everything by so doing: his beloved son, his future as a progenitor of the race, his daily happiness. And what could he see that he might get? Nothing!

This moral equation became Abraham's ultimate test, the final proof (in the story) as to whether he is admirable, lovable, worthy of our reader concern. In such stories, we writhe in agony with the character facing such a dilemma.

Abraham, you will recall from the Bible, tried to delay a decision about his dilemma. God would have none of it, and demanded a decision at once. At this moment, Abraham became the sum total of who and what he was, and made no speeches, consulted no standard references, gave no sermons, but simply showed his decision in action.

He raised his hand to slay his beloved son, Isaac.

At which point his Hebrew onlookers must have been filled with love and admiration and horror. After all, here Abraham was, doing the right thing, and he was surely about to lose everything.

Such a moment of horror and fear in the reader is the ultimate goal of the writer at the climax. We know now that the character is admirable and deserving. He has proven it. But in this dark moment after the decision, it appears he will lose all precisely because he has made the right choice, given us the morally and spiritually uplifting and affirmative answer to his story equation:

$$\text{Parental love} + \text{Love of God} = \text{Love of God}$$

But now, says Foster-Harris, if Abraham slays his son and loses all, then what has the story proved about the human condition? That good choices mean nothing; that life is random and cruel; that selfishness is better than principle. And none of that is good because most fiction, based on a moral equation, is at some level an affirmation of traditional values and a statement that life is worth living truly and honestly and that good is rewarded. Art, like religion, is life affirming.

Therefore—as in the story of Abraham—there must be a *reversal*.

In the Bible story, God stays Abraham's hand. He says it was a test of Abraham's love for Him.

So we breathe a sigh of relief at this reversal of our expectations, this unforeseen turn of events. Isaac is spared. And then we think, "But of course! I didn't see it before, but Abraham's God would never have really asked him to sacrifice Isaac! I should have seen that it was a test!" The sacrificial decision is followed by a dark moment, which is followed by a reversal, which is both *logical and unanticipated*. And this in itself is tremendously satisfying.

But note, please, that the ancient teller of the Abraham tale did not stop there. Abraham not only gets what he thought he was about to lose—his son—but God tells him, in effect, that since he has proven his great love for God, God will name him to lead His people, and his seed will endure forever.

Kingship and immortality.

Rewards far beyond Abraham's wildest dreams—and far more than he thought he would have if he earlier chose the "bad" decision about sacrificing Isaac—and all because he made the right instinctive choice.

So life and decency are affirmed, and the human condition validated.

All novels may not work with plot and character materials that lend themselves to a climax involving sacrifice and reversal. But if you will analyze any dozen popular novels on the stands, you are sure to find elements of sacrifice by the major character *throughout* the novel. In at least half of those books, the climax will involve the viewpoint character with his back to the wall; forced to an ultimate, cruel moral dilemma (which illustrates the equation); making a decision shown in action (which makes the decision concrete and dramatic). There will be a dark moment (which shakes the reader's confidence), and a reversal that is simply wonderfully satisfying (bringing out the affirmative theme).

In bad fiction, you can see that the plot and people have been manipulated to bring about the desired end. In good fiction, it seems inevitable.

What's the difference? Author skill and hard work.

Look at your plot materials, how you plan to end your story. Find the ultimate test. Set up the background and the character goals, needs and assumptions so that, hidden inside the seeming disaster, lie the fruits of glory. Play the scene for all it's worth—which is everything, since this is your ultimate proof that the character is worth saving. And then bring out your theme, without preaching, by showing the dynamic reversal of expectations, both the character's, and your reader's.

The process is fundamental to how we learn all the most significant things in our life. Fantasy, some think, is the process by which we remember our yesterdays, and story is the process by which we create a unity out of the chaos of existence.

Does the idea of a happy ending worry you? It needn't. People read for affirmation, inspiration, escape, assurance that life is basically worth living—at least some of the time—and they do not read to learn more about the humdrum, the routine, the dull, or the discouraging. None of those things are what art is about. So you needn't worry, and your ending needn't be phony if you exercise your judgment, compassion and skill.

You may assuage your worry about happy endings by turning the equation upside down, by showing a less-than-admirable character making the selfish choice in order to win everything. And then, of course, that character loses because, hidden in the situation, were the seeds of destruction he could not see through his selfishness.

Let me repeat: all stories are not told this way, but most of the best ones are.

Consider the implications of the philosophical point of view and its technical implications. Don't, please, think you're too cynical, smart, worldly wise or sophisticated to use as best you can this view of how a story ends. For surely by now you understand that smart sophisticates never write good novels. They are all too busy being superior to their readers.

In the next chapter we'll talk more about story development and endings. But this is enough for you to chew on for the moment.

Take a day off. Think about it.

8

Scene and Sequel

Gut-level understanding
of scene and sequel
is the single most crucial factor
in becoming a successful novelist.

Dwight V. Swain has retired as a full-time teacher of professional writing technique. His book, *Techniques of the Selling Writer,** remains one of the best ever written on all aspects of story writing. I recommend it to you.

It was Swain, many years ago, who pounded scene structure at me in individual conferences over a period of three years. He kept telling me the same thing, and I kept assuring him I *understood perfectly,* then I kept going off and writing more chapters, which proved again and again that I only imagined I understood.

Swain, bless him, kept on pounding.

Finally I saw the light. I still remember the flash of insight.

---

*Techniques of the Selling Writer by Dwight V. Swain.

"So that's what he's been saying!" I cried. And went off and wrote a novel that sold. And fourteen more in succession.

Swain's book is wonderful on scene and sequel structure. But since he writes almost telegraphically at times—and because recalcitrant students have forced me to expand a bit on his theory—I write this chapter with these suggestions:

1. Consult Swain's book as well as mine, because hearing the theory in different words may help you learn this faster than I did.

2. Don't kiss scene and sequel off with the comment, "I understand it." Because unless you've sold several novels, you undoubtedly don't!

3. Give this chapter several readings. Without learning what is in this chapter, I would never have sold more than 60 novels. In fact, I probably would never have been published.

Do I have your attention? I hope so. Because this, dear reader, is for me the heart of the matter: *dramatic structure*.

People read novels to escape the reality of their everyday, humdrum, sometimes-depressing lives. They look for entertainment, thought-provoking ideas, colorful locales, involvement with the story people through their imagination.

To put it in a word, readers read for excitement of some kind.

To provide the reader with excitement, you have to have a story to tell. You have to have good characters. You have to have feeling. But above all else you have to have a *storytelling structure* that provides a lifelike reading experience.

Four characteristics of our experience of real life are:

1. It is lived moment by moment, with no summary.
2. It is lived from a single viewpoint.
3. It is lived now.
4. It is lived with the knowledge that what we do has results.

Therefore, it seems only logical that we would want to put as much of our novel as possible in the same kind of framework.

That's why we have scene: a component of the story that plays out in the story now, from a single viewpoint, told moment by moment, with no summary, and in a way so that what the characters do has downstream impact on the course of the rest of the story.

A problem, however, immediately becomes apparent. If we try to tell *all* of our novel moment by moment, even the shortest tale will become hopelessly long. Writing down an entire hour of your life, even a dull hour, with *no summary of any kind* might fill a volume. And in real life we sort of summarize by daydreaming, nodding off, or not paying attention for a while.

So everything in a novel cannot be a scene.

That's one of the reasons we have the other component of story, the sequel.

When we talk about scene and sequel, we are talking about a very specific structure and method of attacking the story material. So let's look at them one at a time.

▪▪ SCENE STRUCTURE ▪▪

Scene provides excitement, involvement. Its structure is threefold: *goal, conflict, disaster.*

Just as a story starts with statement of a character's long-term goal, so every scene starts with a character, the viewpoint character, saying very specifically what he wants to accomplish in the confrontation that is about to take place. This subsidiary goal relates—is a steppingstone somehow—to the long-term story goal. So just as the reader forms a story question from story goal, and worries about it, he also forms a *scene question,* realizes the link between this stated secondary goal and the big goal, and worries about the scene question, too.

The scene goal can be stated by having the character say it out loud beforehand:

> "Mickey, I'm going in there and I have *got* to convince Bigley to let me off early so I can go to night school two nights a week."

Or it can be stated in character thought:

> Walking into Bigley's office, Cliff knew he had to convince Bigley to let him off early two nights a week.

Or it can be stated or paraphrased in the opening lines of the scene after earlier notice to the reader:

> "Mister Bigley, I'm here to convince you that it's vital for me to get off work early two nights a week. I think it will be a good thing for the company, too."

Sometimes (although without elaboration this is risky), the goal can be decided in what preceded the scene, so that the reader understands clearly what the goal is all about. But please notice this: however the specific, short-term goal is stated, it must be absolutely clear to the reader!

Good novelists never write a scene where the goal is vague or ambiguous. They never make the mistake of trying to be subtle about it. The reader has to know what's wanted in no uncertain terms. So good writers leave no doubt about it. They write so that the goal in every scene is *perfectly clear, specific,* and *obtainable now.*

It's obvious, but so many new writers would like to be subtle or clever, when all one needs to do is to be clear and specific. This is no place to be subtle.

Imagine that the next time you went to a football game, you climbed into the stands and were confronted by an endless gridiron, extending over the horizon to the south on your right, the north on your left. Time would come for the start of the game, and maybe the kickoff would come within your field of vision. But then suppose the opposing team mounted a drive—and drove right out of sight to the north.

You would sit and wait, totally uninvolved and confused.

Maybe a little later you would see one of the home team's halfbacks churn over the far horizon, chug past the stands, and then disappear over the horizon to the south.

"What is this?" you would cry. "I don't know what's going on! This is crazy! I'm getting out of here!"

Why? No goals in sight. So the game could not possibly make sense.

That's the way it works in a scene, too. The goal must be stated specifically, clearly.

What about the conflict part of the scene? Actually, it's 95–98 percent of it. Once the goal has been stated, someone has to come along at once and say, in effect, "Huh-uh. You're not getting that, and I'm here to stop you." This antagonist, too, is strongly motivated because he sees how this scene fits into his book-long struggle against the hero, how the outcomes of this confrontation fit into *his* game plan. And so a struggle starts.

How is it developed? Moment by moment, with no summary. Like real life.

How do you develop moment by moment?

Through stimulus and response transactions.

The two fighters feint and parry, maneuver, try variations of their game plan, try to gain advantage, reveal their character in what they say and do under pressure, and fight to win.

Finally all the maneuvers have been tried, and the scene is to end.

How does it end?

If Cliff goes into Bigley's office intent on getting permission to leave early two nights a week, should we end the scene with his getting what he came after?

Absolutely not! In storytelling terms, good news is always bad tactics, bad news always good. After all, if events in this novel have downstream effects, and everything is tied tightly together, and the goal in this scene relates to Cliff's story quest, then (if he gets this goal) he's happy, everything is going fine, he's on his way to getting what he wants in the long run, and there is no reader suspense or tension.

And maybe the story just ended.

So the scene cannot end well for poor Cliff. There must be a setback—a disaster.

What is a disaster? It's a logical but unanticipated turn of events by which Cliff, by struggling to attain something good and worthwhile, and *as a result of having tried so hard,* gets anything but what he wants.

So as a result of having struggled manfully he is farther behind the eight ball than ever.

"This is awful!" the reader thinks. "I feel bad for Cliff! I feel sorry for him! Damn, I want him to win, but I don't think he can, now! I feel terrible and filled with suspense!

"What a great novel this is!"

To work well, however, the disaster cannot just be any bad news the lazy writer wants to shovel in.

Suppose Cliff goes in and tells Bigley he wants time off. Bigley says no. They argue and maneuver. At the end, you need a disaster. So you have somebody rush in and say the plant is on fire.

No, no, no.

No good at all.

Why? Because this disaster is an alligator over the transom. It has nothing to do with the fight that just took place.

To work, the disaster must be organic. That is, it must grow logically out of what has been going on in the scene.

To put it another way: every scene starts with a goal, and the goal statement raises a scene question in the reader's mind. This question must always be one which can be answered simply in terms of the goal. The only possible answers are:

yes; no; yes, but; or *no, and furthermore.*

We've already seen that, while possible, the "yes" answer destroys all reader tension and probably kills off your story because the hero is suddenly fat, dumb, happy, and on his way to see the Wizard. So the scene question has to be answered "No," "Yes, but!," or "No, and furthermore!" And this answer has to be logical but unanticipated, and it has to put the viewpoint character in a worse position.

Want an example? Fine. Let's look at poor Cliff again.

Suppose that a central value of Cliff's life is that he must be a good provider for his young sister, whom he supports. His concept of himself is of a responsible, hard-working older brother. His entire life script* centers around being a good provider and fulfilling family responsibilities.

Cliff has decided that, in order to be this person, he has to have a good office job with Bigley Wrench Company. But to get a good office job, he has to become an accountant. In order to become an accountant, he has to go to night school. In order to go to night school, he has to have two evenings off early each week. In order to get the time off, he has to convince Bigley.

So he goes into this meeting dedicated to his goal. And it all ties together. This is mandatory!

He tells Bigley what he wants. Bigley demurs. Cliff argues fervently. Bigley grows irritated. Seeing his dream slipping away, Cliff presses the fight, becoming eloquent. The two men struggle, argue, maneuver.

Finally comes the climax of the scene. We want a disaster.

We can have Bigley say:

"Cliff, I've heard enough! For the last time, my answer is *no!* Now get out of this office!"

---

*We're assuming things here that we haven't talked about yet in this book. You may want to make a marker here, and refer back to these aspects of Cliff's motivation after reading about characterization in later chapters.

Fine, you say.

Yes, it's good. But not great.

Why? Because, when you examine the situation, Cliff leaves *in no worse shape than when he went in*. Not much has changed. His problem has grown no worse. He is no more desperate, in no additional trouble. There really hasn't been much dramatic "progress."

So a "no" answer is good, but often you need even more than that.

Let's play the scene again. Same stuff. At the end, let's have Bigley become cunning and say:

> "Okay, Cliff. I'm not convinced. But let's put it this way. I'm a reasonable man. My answer is *yes, but* you have to work twelve hours both Saturdays and Sundays to make up for it. Which means you'll never get to spend any time with your sister, or studying."

This is better. Did Cliff get what he wanted? Yes, but! He staggered out of the office in worse shape, and with more problems, than when he went in to fight the good fight.

A lot of scenes end this way in working fiction. Usually they have the added impact of giving Cliff some new scene or series of scenes (new plot) as he tries to cope with the dimensions of the new and unexpected disaster.

But perhaps there is even a stronger way.

Same scene. Bigley gets more and more impatient, finally angry. At the end he shouts:

> "Damn it, Cliff! For the tenth time, the answer is *no! And furthermore*, you have made me so angry with your arguing that I've had it with you. You've pushed me too far. You're fired!"

All right! Now we've done something really good. Cliff staggers out a wreck, having lost everything because he tried to work toward a worthwhile goal. He brought on his own disaster. He not only failed to reach the short-term laudable goal, but he made his situation worse. Now he has no job—which really threatens his self-concept as a good breadwinner.

This is "progress."

The best and most dramatic scenes work like this.

We make our story go forward by pushing our hero backward, farther and farther from his ultimate goal, through scene disaster. The reader reads excitedly, roots for the hero—then is crushed with him. The novel flies along, lifelike, dramatic, suspenseful, hard to put down, filled with twists, surprises and setbacks—and more and more tension as well as admiration for the battered hero who simply won't quit.

▪▪ SEQUEL ▪▪

What happens with Cliff as he leaves Bigley's factory for the last time?

> "My God!" he cries, clapping his hand to his forehead. "I feel shocked and scared and angry and terrible! What can I possibly do now? No avenue looks good! I've got to think about this... let me see... I guess I'll go down the street and try to get a job at Acme Tool." And he starts down the street.

And that, in a nutshell, is the pattern of sequel: *emotion, quandary, decision, action.*

This is the way we react to any disaster in real life. First: blind emotional reaction. Later, a struggle to think again, but confusion, where possibly no course of action looks very good. Finally, a new decision, maybe not very good, but the best we can come up with. And then new action based on that decision.

The nature of scene is excitement. But the nature of sequel is logic, with emotion and characterization thrown in.

Sequel allows summary, transition, skipped time. It is where the character reacts to what just took place (the disaster), looks at his hole card, plans something next to try, and gets going again.

Some sequels may be as short as the one we imagined poor old Cliff going through moments ago. Some may go on forever. Scene is swift-moving and involving, but there isn't a lot of time for thought, except for stimulus-response internalizations. Sequel is slow-moving and possibly emotional, and there is time for thought and feeling.

In a slam-bang action adventure novel, the entire sequel, after the mad killer hits the hero on the head with a meat-ax, might be something like this:

> Bart's skull hurt like hell. "Damn, that makes me mad!" Bart thought. "I'm going to kill that sucker!" And he hurled himself back into the fight.

Such a book reads breathlessly, at a wild pace, never a letup.

In a novel like *Herzog*,* on the other hand, Amos Herzog spends most of a long book in sequel to a scene or scenes that played *before* the novel ever opened. The result is a long, lovely, thoughtful, evocative book.

So how you handle sequel depends on the fictional situation, your intent as a writer, your authorial bent and architectonic demands of the moment, in view of the pace of your entire novel's structure.

We can, however, make some points about each segment of the sequel, even if you must decide how long any section should be—and, indeed, whether some sections are to play out on the page at all.

The first part of the natural reaction cycle is *emotion*. Pure feeling, with little thought possible just yet. This period may

---

*Herzog by Saul Bellow.

be as brief as it is in the exaggerated example about Bart just above; or it may extend for many story hours, days or weeks, many manuscript pages or chapters.

The length of time devoted to the emotional reaction will depend on the kind of character you're writing about, and the kind of plot. A tough, self-disciplined Marine Corps officer might allow himself very little emotion, and if he were in an action story where you had to get on with the plot, the emotion portion of the sequel might be very brief indeed. On the other hand, a highly emotional woman in a love story, where the reader interest is centered precisely on emotion, might be given many pages of sensitive rendition of her feelings.

The emotional segment of the sequel, like its other parts, may be rendered by the author's getting into the character's heart, and describing the feelings directly. The description of emotion might be more cool, almost clinical, as the author backed away a bit from trying to describe the feelings directly. It might be portrayed by having the sequel character talk with another story person and tell how she is feeling. You'll find examples of each approach in your writing. I hope you'll look for them, mark them, and make notes of your findings and impressions in your work journal.

Writing the emotion segment of sequel is the most dangerous place for the writer who tends to get carried away and write purple, hysterical prose. Therefore, many contemporary writers tend to cool their approach to emotion in sequel, and press on as quickly as possible.

A person overwhelmed by emotion is always either paralyzed or acting crazy. Neither state moves the story forward very much. For this reason, too, the emotional compartment of the sequel has to end at some point, and the character has to start thinking again..

This *quandary* section usually takes the form of: *review, options*, and *search*.

The character thinks, in effect, "I've got to review what this disaster means and how it came about, look at my options, and search for a new course of action to get my quest back on track somehow." Not all three parts are always played, and, as in other parts of the sequel, the process may be short or long depending on circumstance.

Following a disaster, the character prototypically reviews not only how the last disaster took place but what it means; in doing this, sometimes a review of high points earlier in the plot may be necessary. These often-painful reviews by the view-point character put things in perspective for the reader, too, and are wonderful focusing devices that keep the long-term story question in clear view, and point out what's significant.

After reviewing, the character starts looking at new options, and is struck by a dilemma, that of seeing two possible courses of (new) action, neither of which looks very good. More often, the dilemma quickly becomes a *quandary* as—with the character—you the author show the thought process by which the character explores all possible new goal-oriented actions.

This is the place where your character really plots the next stage of your novel for you. She considers doing this, or that, but finds problems with both. Then she thinks of other avenues she might try.

Having considered a lengthy list of what really are author plot development options, she starts searching through them to find the one that looks best. Her thought processes, courage (or lack of it), ingenuity, demonstrated devotion to the cause, and intelligence all characterize her as she searches on.

Finally—perhaps in a page, perhaps in thirty of them—she makes her new *decision*. She selects what she will do, and commits to this new plan and goal.

She moves into her newly chosen plan. She goes some-where and does something, and reiterates her newly chosen goal. Someone confronts her in conflict—

And where are you?

In the next scene.

Scene leads to sequel leads to scene leads to sequel. *This is the structure of long fiction that tells a story.*

And of course from my biased standpoint there is no other kind.

People will argue that everything that happens in a novel is not a scene, and that every feeling thoughtful passage is not a sequel. This is true; there are incidents without real meaning —with no downstream effects—in a novel. The fewer of these there are, however, the better the novel is likely to be. Accomplished novelists can turn almost all their incidents or accidental encounters into little scenes, at least, with subtle disasters or twists at the end. You can too, if you will try.

The key to turning already written, dead incidents into dramatic scenes often lies in searching back to the opening of your existing incident and searching for an implied intention on the part of the viewpoint character. Then it may be possible to emphasize, clarify, and finally thwart this intention in the incident's conclusion, turning it into the basis for a scene.

Here's an example:

I once had a friend who wrote a long incident involving a schoolteacher with high school kids on a tour abroad. The way she wrote it, the woman had the bus driver take them to a big castle on the hill, as planned in the tour book. When the bus arrived, the woman got off, went to the door, and met a cranky, sinister, older man who said they could stay the night as planned, but wouldn't enjoy it.

This sequence of events seemed flat and undramatic. It just sort of sat there on the page.

Why? Because it was mere incident.

I suggested to my friend that she make the sequence into a scene.

"I don't write scenes!" she wailed. "I can't!"

After we fixed that self-concept problem, her revision was cast like this:

Same basic situation, same heroine. But now, the heroine noticed, as the bus approached the castle, that some of the kids were nervous and cranky, perhaps scared of the old castle. So the heroine *formed the intention* of persuading them that staying the night would be fun. With this goal in mind, she walked up to the door of the castle. When the sinister man appeared, she stated her goal and urged him to help her reassure the kids by coming down to the bus and talking to them. The man argued; she insisted. Finally he marched down to the bus and said, in effect, "There's nothing to worry about. The police believe that the man who killed seven students here last week is no longer in the immediate area."

The goal was: *Get the man to talk to the kids*.

The question then became: *Will she get the man to talk to the kids?*

And the disaster thus became: *Yes, BUT as a result of her efforts, he came down and scared all of them—including her—a lot more*.

So the heroine marched into the castle feeling much worse than she would have if she hadn't tried anything at all, and as a result of that (in sequel), decided to take the kids on a fun sidetrip the next day, but...

I hope you begin to get the picture.

Developing good, disastrous scenes will tax your ingenuity. It will also *make* your novel. Writing good sequels will put you and the reader in closer touch with the character, and lay out future developments in the novel, while also, perhaps, patching up story logic and motivation.

Scenes, remember, are fast and involving. They make the story fly. Sequels are slower by nature, slowing down the pace of your story. Therefore, it stands to reason that *you control the pace of your story by scene and sequel*.

If the story is too breakneck, you lengthen a sequel.

If it's going too slowly, you expand scenes, shorten or even leave out sequels.

Other vital points about scene and sequel:

1. Scene and sequel do not have to be played in the chronological order they were planned.

2. Scene can interrupt sequel, and vice versa.

3. A scene or sequel may be skipped entirely.

4. Scene-sequel structure is the key to how (and when) you change viewpoint.

5. Understanding of scene structure is the key to writing copy that's hard to put down.

Let's take a look at these additional important points:

Scene and sequel need not be—and indeed seldom are—presented to the reader in the chronological order that the writer imagined and planned them.

The beginning writer tends to tell his story in summary, the way we report an interesting event in conversation. Most of the time, we also tell such oral stories chronologically, in the time order in which the events took place.

One of the first things a fiction writer has to learn, however, is that straight summary is not involving enough for readers. As we have seen, some events must be developed moment by moment and put on stage, as it were, for dramatic impact on the reader's imagination.

This discovery—of the need for dramatic presentation alternating with periods of introspection—eventually leads the writer to some understanding of scene and sequel structure. And what a day that is, because suddenly everything begins to make sense in terms of how to put long stories together!

Even at this stage in the writer's development, however, she often tends to present her scenes and sequels just as she first imagined and collated them: Monday, Tuesday, Wednesday, 9 A.M., 1 P.M., 6 P.M.

This can be deadly because actually presenting the story in straight chronology often leads to a story that plods, gets predictable, is too even and boring, and doesn't have the surprises and dramatic peaks that it otherwise might have.

Even worse, there's a serious danger that the reader may figure out how she is being tricked into breathless suspense and gut-wrenching emotion through the structure. We can't have that.

Although you plan your story from the first action on day one to the last action on the last day, you seldom if ever present it that way.

It may be, for example, that your novel outline shows hero Andy meeting his mistress (scene 1); realizing he is in love with her and agonizing over what he is to do about his marriage (sequel 1); going to the bank and tricking the banker into letting him withdraw all the money from a joint account (scene 2); worrying about his trickery as he heads home (sequel 2); confronting his wife with the truth of his behavior and feelings (scene 3); feeling bad as he moves out (sequel 3); meeting his mistress to cheer himself up but learning that her plans definitely do not include living with him on a committed basis (scene 4); feeling really horrible (sequel 4); while you as the author know that at the same time Andy is seeing his mistress and learning the horrible truth, his wife is going to the bank and finding out that their life savings have been withdrawn (scene 5); has thought about it (sequel 5); and has called the police and convinced them to arrest Andy (scene 6). Which they then do (scene 7).

Even this simple sequence of events can't be played chronologically. If you do, there are at least two things wrong: the reader won't be surprised with the wife when she learns the money is missing (because we already slavishly played that little bit when Andy did it earlier), and we're in trouble when we try to be chronological with events that our planning charts show are happening at the same time.

What to do? Obviously, play the scenes and sequels for better dramatic effect, clarity, and mystery.

Possibly you open with Andy's viewpoint as he confronts his wife, and the reader is immediately plunged into a harrowing scene between them. (You have skipped several things already.) Perhaps then you skip time to show Andy's wife making her discovery at the bank, and angrily dialing a number—the police, as you know, but you withhold this information from the reader for more suspense. Then perhaps you show Andy learning the bitter truth from the mistress, and in his sequel to that, you have him review his earlier dreams, and play in his review the earlier meeting he had with the woman in which he knew he loved her. Then, perhaps, you have him finish the sequel and walk outside and be arrested, and the next thing we know, two days have passed and his sequel to all this has been put out of order so we can leap straight to another scene between him and his wife, or him and his lawyer.

So that what you *planned* was:

> Scene 1
> Sequel 1
> Scene 2
> Sequel 2
> Scene 3
> Sequel 3
> Scene 4
> Sequel 4
> Scene 5
> Sequel 5
> Scene 6

But what you *played* for the reader was:

> Scene 3
> Scene 5
> Scene 6
> Scene 4
> Sequel 4
> Scene 1
> Sequel 1
> Scene 7

The result of such rearrangement of scene and sequel is that the reader gets the big moments in the order in which maximum impact will be derived, at the same time being kept constantly off balance.

Another example, from a published work, may clarify things further.

In her novel *The Trembling Hills*,* Phyllis A. Whitney takes us to the brink of a scene in which the young heroine is about to walk into a room and confront an aged and formidable matriarch with information about their blood kinship. The female narrator is scared about the scene now to unfold, and we are on edge. The girl walks into the room to face the old woman— and the chapter ends.

We turn the page, breathless to see the scene unfold, and find ourselves at a family dinner many hours later, with the principals talking about something else altogether!

We read well into this considerably later scene before the narrator says, in effect, "It had been harrowing, facing my grandmother, but when I had walked into the room that afternoon I had said . . ." This turns the female narrator's mind to a small sequel to something that had just played onstage during the evening dinner. She reviews, in this sequel, the scene that had taken place earlier in the day, and plays that scene inside this later sequel for us now. Then she goes on—still in the mid-dinner sequel—to play for us the earlier sequel she had had after the earlier scene!

Whitney has been one of our cleverest writers for decades, and this technique has worked wonderfully—puzzling us, compelling us forward, and deepening a sequence of events that might not have been nearly as fascinating if told chronologically.

A note of warning about this technique, however. You must *never* delay a big scene like this unless you are very clear in your mind that drama will be *increased* by your playing of it out of normal order.

I note this because writers sometimes inadvertently skip or delay big scenes because they will be hard to write, and for no

---

**The Trembling Hills* by Phyllis A. Whitney

other reason. So if you use this device, use it with good reason, and not to make things easier on yourself as writer.

If you think about this, study your own work, and analyze published novels, you'll quickly see that scene and sequel are always there, but—if the story is effective—often are invisible to the reader because they are not played one after the other, like link sausages.

Scene can interrupt sequel, and vice versa.

One example of why this is so: In a novel I wrote many years ago, called *Katie, Kelly and Heck,** there was a point early on in the book where I needed to motivate an essentially cautious and intelligent heroine to get mildly involved with a man who was obviously, in the language of the story era, a "bounder and a cad." How was I to do this?

First I set up a simmering animosity between Katie and another man in the story, Mike Kelly. Then I introduced my humorously oily villain, the other man, Ray Root, in a scene in which he asked Katie to go out with him. During this scene, Mike Kelly then rushed in, and tried to have his scene with Katie. So the Mike scene interrupted the Root scene. As a later result of which, Katie—to end her scene with Mike and spite him just as viciously as she could—recklessly turned back to Ray Root and accepted his invitation to go out.

So the Mike scene functioned as motive for Katie to do something stupid in the other scene, which it interrupted. You'll find many other examples once you start looking for them.

A scene or sequel may be skipped entirely. Three scenes may come one after the other so rapidly that the viewpoint character simply has no time for a developed sequel between them. Or, for surprise, you may skip a scene entirely to get on to an even bigger one.

You may *plan* it: scene 1, sequel 1, scene 2, sequel 2, scene

---

*Katie, Kelly and Heck by Jack M. Bickham.

3, sequel 3, for example. Whereas you may actually *present* it: scene 1, scene 2, sequel 2, sequel 3, or in any other skipped order that enhances the dramatic effect.

But you still will have had to plan them all in order to have the materials which you can skip or meddle with for greater effect.

Action-adventure stories often skip many sequels. Deeply psychological novels and many "literary" books often skip many scenes. That doesn't mean they're not all there, in the planning. They're simply not all played, depending on the writer's intentions and the effects she wishes to produce.

Scene-sequel structure is the key to how (and when) you change viewpoint, if you choose to do so at all. Within either component, you will have a far easier time of it (and so will your reader) if you maintain the same viewpoint until the end of that structural component.

If you decide to change viewpoint at, say, the moment of scene-closing disaster, you can go to other viewpoints and insert a transition of many days or even months—and move the action halfway across the globe—and still bring the reader back to the original viewpoint clearly and without pain if you maintain structural integrity and *pick the character up again where you left him structurally.*

This is what I mean: suppose you have a scene in which Reggie insists that the bank examiner reveal who stole the funds. At the end, the examiner says, "Okay, Reggie, I wanted to spare you this. But the thief is your missing brother."

Wham! Nice disaster. Nice place to change viewpoint. So you do so, going perhaps to the missing brother, to the hero's wife, or to the bank examiner. A week passes. You as the author know that the hero, while offstage for other viewpoints, has gone from Oklahoma City to London, England.

Big transition. Can the reader handle it?

Sure. If you maintain structural integrity.

Think: where did we leave Reggie?

At the disaster.

So where must we pick him up, to keep things straight in the reader's mind?

At the start of his sequel to that disaster, of course.

So we come back to Reggie with a statement like:

Reggie was still reeling from shock and humiliation a week later as his British taxi stopped in front of London's Cumberland Hotel.

The reader has no problem whatsoever with the transition across time and space because—in terms of structure—*nothing has happened to Reggie.* He is exactly where he would have been if his viewpoint line had been followed up immediately after the disaster.

Readers don't understand scene and sequel. But oh, do they have a sense of it. And that sense—their almost intuitive grasp of story structure—makes changes of point of view and gaping transitions not only possible but easy as pie.

This is why scene and sequel structure are the key to writing copy that's hard to put down. You leave a viewpoint at a disaster, go to another character and put her in a similar disaster moment, switch back to the first and get his reaction to the first disaster and show him walking into a likely new disaster, switch back to the other character and take her to the point of decision and then leave her viewpoint again with a line such as, "Then she knew what she had to do. . . ." and change viewpoint again, leaving the reader hanging as to what the character's new decision is. Now you've got copy that keeps the reader turning the pages like crazy, being tricked again and again into suspense and worry.

The best place to change viewpoint is at the disaster. Second-best, probably, is at the moment of new decision in the sequel, whether or not you choose to hold out on the reader as to what that decision is. Third-best is during the decision-making process, when the character struggles with quandary.

A case could be made, in some books, for the best spot of all being midway in the emotional hell of the sequel, if you're writing a book where the sequel really is hell, where you get deep into the character's emotions.

We'll talk more of scene and sequel later. For now, let me urge you to read many novels and mark them up, in order to engrain the patterns in your mind and heart.

Mark, say, the goal statement in red

The conflict section in blue brackets

Steps in that conflict (as goals shift subtly) in yellow

The disaster in green

And each step of the sequel in other colors

Note if parts of the sequel are not played. Ask yourself why. If viewpoints change, note when and where, and ask yourself why. When a viewpoint returns to the stage, is structural integrity maintained? How?

Practice planning scenes and sequels. Think in scenes and sequels.

There's nothing more important for a novelist.

If you take a week or two off right now, read no more, and work like hell on this single chapter and its implications, wonderful.

Have I made the point?

This chapter is the heart and soul of storytelling.

9

Handling Time

*There are three kinds of time
in a novel:
reader time,
story time,
and writer time.
And the novelist has to control them all.*

An odd fact often becomes apparent to the novelist about the time his first book is published: there is no relationship between the time he takes to write a story and the time it may take a reader to read it.

Once, after spending many months of intense labor on a relatively short novel, I saw this fact most clearly when I read the first review published on the work. The reviewer said something like: *"This is an enjoyable two-evening read, with lots of suspense."*

"Wait a minute!" I thought in distress. "That makes it sound like I wrote the thing in a couple of evenings."

It's obvious that the amount of time you spend working on a book will have no relationship to the amount of time the reader may invest in reading it. (It may even be in inverse proportion: the longer you work on the yarn, the faster it will be read.)

This can be discouraging, and the source of an additional problem for the writer. Why? Because you must always try to be aware of the *reader's* pace and time, not your own. To put it another way, you must never be confused by the amount of time you may put in on creating a scene or chapter, because writer time is invisible to the reader. If you start thinking that a segment that took you long to write will take a reader long to read, then the pacing of your novel may get all out of whack.

You may, for example, labor mightily for two or three days revising a transitional page of copy which is supposed to give the reader the sense of a month's time passing in the narrative. But just because you invested a lot of time in the creation, you cannot assume the reader will be slowed down, and get the desired sense of narrative time going by. But if you then look at your passage coldly, and calculate what's going on in terms of time, you may come up with something like this:

Story time—one month
Writer time—three days
Reader time—two minutes

What to do? Awareness of the phenomenon is the critical factor. Once you see clearly that there's no necessary relationship between the times, you can discard entirely any awareness of how long it took you to create a segment; that's an author problem that nobody else cares about. As to building in some kind of relationship between story time and reader time, you do it by recognizing a couple of basic narrative principles, then by controlling the pace through selection of your mode of discourse.

▪▪ NARRATIVE PRINCIPLES ▪▪

The more intense the pressure, the more slowly and minutely you cover the action or thought, moment by moment, with nothing left out. These high points, then, may represent only minutes in story time, but, paradoxically, may require more reader time than the passage of a year somewhere else in the story.

To put this another way, the bigger the scene, the longer the reader time.

When something conflictful is happening, the reader reads faster. Therefore, the long sequence described just above, which may require a lot of reader time, may seem to the reader to go at lightning speed, and may seem to require no time at all.

Moments of meditation and review (sequel) tend to read more slowly. Therefore, even a relatively short sequel passage may give the reader the effect of slowing down, passing a lot of time.

Conclusion: You can control the pace of your novel in large part by the juggling of scene and sequel. Even the longest scene reads swiftly and seems to rush along in little reader time. Even a brief sequel slows her down, relaxes some of her tensions, and gives the impression of more of her (reader) time passing.

If your story is going too slowly, build your scenes and shorten your sequels.

If your story is going too swiftly (and thoughtlessly), trim your scenes or build up your sequels.

This is the key to giving your novel "peaks and valleys." I heard about peaks and valleys from English professors for years, and never could find one of the damned things. That's because it makes no more sense to speak of peaks and valleys in fiction than it does to say a story has a beginning, a middle, and an end. What does that mean? So does a dachshund!

What we're really talking about, when we talk about peaks and valleys, is the fact that the reader sometimes needs a break between big scenes so that two scenes won't detract from each other by their close proximity. Sometimes (in another kind of book) the reader needs some present, swifter-moving action to intensify, by contrast, the solitary mood of the sequel when we get back to it.

You manipulate reader time for dramatic purposes, and to reflect in the most general way the time scheme of the novel.

So much for general principles.

How else can you vary and control narrative pace?

By understanding modes of discourse.

Let's look at them and note their characteristics.

■ ■ NARRATION ■ ■

The fastest-moving of them all. Here the writer tells what's happening in somewhat condensed form, just as economically as she can write it. It whizzes along at breakneck speed—rushes the reader forward with the impression of practically no time (for the reader) passing.

Example:

I left the office, hurried down the stairs, and got behind the wheel of the car. Moments later I hit the turnpike and put the accelerator to the floor, the big engine whining, the speedometer climbing toward 100. I reached Joplin at noon, St. Louis less than four hours later—confronted Slade in his office at six.

Narration is used when speedy transition between scenes is needed, when the writer wants to hurry the story along, when something dramatic is happening, but doesn't lend itself to scene structure. When you write narration, your artistic distance from the story may be considerable and you may even get out of viewpoint. But the pace is incredible. To be used with care.

■ ■ DRAMATIC ACTION ■ ■

Next to the swiftest, this is the stuff of scene. Give and take, stimulus and response, action onstage now, with no summary. Example:

I stepped into the dark room. Couldn't see a thing. Heard the slightest rustle of movement somewhere near the desk and knew he was here. I slid along the wall to my right. Get behind him, I thought. My foot touched something and betrayed my movement and there was a bright orange burst of light across the room and a simultaneous deafening crash and something slammed into my shoulder, knocking me backward with shocking impact. Pain filled me. I heard him coming around the desk. Desperate, I rolled...

Whether you are in such violent physical confrontation in some of your scenes, or something much quieter, the intensity level is much the same. Lots of reader time may be devoted to the minute examination of every instant of story time. But the effect is involvement, plus speed, speed, speed.

■ ■ DIALOGUE ■ ■

Dialogue is often the stuff of scene, too. It's a story speech, told stimulus and response, with no summary. It, too, goes like gangbusters, but affects the reader as slightly slower and less manic than dramatic action.

Example:

> Harry felt a desperate need to talk about something—anything— to try to ease the tension. "What time is it?" he asked.
>
> "Three o'clock," Dan said.
>
> "And he's supposed to arrive at what time, did you say?"
>
> "Now. Right now." Dan's voice cracked. "You know that as well as I do!"
>
> So much for talk, Harry thought. "Sorry."
>
> "Just shut up, that's all."

There will be more about dialogue in a later chapter. For now, just note that as a mode of discourse it's involving and quite fast-moving.

▪▪ DESCRIPTION ▪▪

This mode orients the reader to the story world, whether the description is of setting, another character's appearance or expression, or even of the viewpoint's internal workings. The key point is that pure description *stops or sharply slows the action* in order to take its look.

Example:

> She was tall, willowy, with legs he would remember forever, he thought. The sunlight backlit her pale hair, made a golden halo around her as she walked toward him. Her sky-blue sundress bared her shoulders and arms. Except for tiny earrings she was innocent of jewelry. Her wide hazel eyes already looked puzzled, even hurt, as he reached toward her.

Although there is a modicum of action here (and I could have built a completely static description for pedagogical effect), the general impact is of *nothing happening*. And when nothing happens, the story creeps or stands still, and reader time seems to slow and even drag. So pure description, or even a variation which allows slight movement during an essentially descriptive passage, will make reader time pass and slow everything down.

▪▪ EXPOSITION ▪▪

Slowest of the modes, exposition is the advancement of straight factual information. Some is essential in every novel. Example:

Joe was thirty-four. He was born in Dallas. He moved to New York after college at SMU. After working three years in a hotel on Park Avenue South, he met a wealthy widow and won her affections sufficiently so that he would never have to work again. He liked big cars. She bought them for him. He spent his afternoons playing bridge.

Bridge is a card game that grew out of a British pastime called whist. Four play in partnerships against one another. The entire pack of fifty-two cards is used. . . .

You will note that this passage moves more clearly into pure exposition with the second paragraph. The first includes elements of narration. Such a mixture of modes is commonplace.

Despite this fact, I want to suggest another exercise to help you clarify your thinking about the modes of discourse. Select a chapter from a current novel. Go through the chapter meticulously and mark:

Narration in red
Dramatic action in orange
Dialogue in yellow
Description in green
Exposition in blue

Having done so, study the pattern of interplay between the modes. What is happening when what mode is used? What was the author's intent here? Do you sense your reactions as a reader speeding or slowing down as you reread the passages?

What can you learn—and apply—from this analysis? Don't be easy on yourself! Force yourself to log at least five positive conclusions in your work journal.

Take your time.

The analysis—and the analytical habits it engrains—will have lifelong benefits.

10

....

Building Characters

*Without sympathetic people
in your story,
you might as well
be writing a grocery list.*

A long time ago, the founder of the Professional Writing Program at the University of Oklahoma said there were eight ways to present a character in fiction:

By action of the character
By speech of the character
By effect of the character on other story people
By the character's reactions to other story people and circumstances
By what other story people say about the character
By explaining traits and motives of the character

By description of the character

By analyzing the psychological processes of the character.*

These observations are as true now as they were then. In this chapter we'll begin talking about some of them.

Before getting to that point, however, another observation seems important to me. And that is this: *exaggeration is the first step toward vivid characters*.

We talked about this much earlier. But it is so important. Time after time I have been confronted by new writers whose novels were peopled with characters who were flat, dull, unclear, uninspiring, uninteresting, and plain old boring. Time after time I have confronted such writers with the bad news: "Your characters simply aren't interesting and realistic enough to engage a reader."

Almost invariably the writer has looked shocked and replied, "But how can that be? These characters are all real people I know!"

This leads to the obvious conclusion about story people that we mentioned much earlier in this book, in our overview: Good characters are not real people; they are better than real people.

They are *exaggerated*.

They are more goal-oriented.

They are more consistent, with tricks used to make them appear complex.

They are engaged in more dramatic circumstances than most of us ever encounter in day-to-day living.

They are closer to symbol, myth and metaphor—the stuff that makes religion sometimes uplift, and makes the best literature approach the status of religious experience.

So in both this chapter and the next we'll look at some fundamental techniques and ideas that may help you build charac-

Writing: Advice and Devices by Walter S. Campbell

ters who are bigger and better than life. For nothing less will do. And if you detect a repetition of advice given earlier in other contexts, maybe you will get an insight into how every technique fits with every other—how the richly textured fabric becomes a whole.

Earlier I explained that fictional characters must be bigger than life—broadly exaggerated in many respects—so that the reader, viewing them as through a smoked glass, can see their salient characteristics. This is fundamental. The real person, translated to paper with total fidelity, will never be seen in the reader's imagination as vivid, clear and unforgettable. So the wise novelist makes the loyal character almost unbelievably loyal, the cruel character horribly cruel, the witty character outrageously brilliant, and so on. Great fictional persons stand on the brink of caricature. And since they are so exaggerated and almost outrageous, the reader sees them through the veil of the reading process as lifelike.

Want a textbook example of exaggeration in character? Go back to the classics, if you wish. There is no better teacher of this technique than Charles Dickens in one of his best works, *Great Expectations*.

If you happen to go too far in exaggerating in your own work, really making your story person too much of a good thing, it is usually possible to tone that character down when the error is pointed out to you. But if you err in the opposite direction, and get far into your book with flat or insipid story people, it's much harder to beef them up. So as you write, it's wise to overstate your story people in the early going. You can always tone them down later if necessary, and chances are good that they may end up just right anyway.

Another advantage to exaggeration of your characters as you write is the fact that the act of exaggeration may stimulate your own imagination in unexpected and wonderful ways.

Many years ago I was writing a western novel that worried me. Halfway through the book, its pace and my own interest seemed to be lagging. Having noticed (and logged the observation in my journal) that my interest in a novel often perked up when a new character came onstage, I decided to introduce a new story person solely for the purpose of adding zest to the tale.

Adding a major character more than halfway through a novel isn't recommended procedure. But I was desperate. So, throwing caution to the winds, I had my marshal riding along a ravine, hearing a great commotion on the far side of the hill, and looking to the hilltop to spy a clamorously exaggerated character.

He was well over six feet tall, that cowboy up there, astraddle a red roan horse and unsteady in the saddle. He was wearing red pants, green shirt, yellow vest, a blue 10-gallon hat, lizard boots with the rowels of his big silver spurs painted purple, and there were crossed shellbelts over his chest. As my marshal stared in disbelief, the cowboy up there tumbled out of his saddle, and he and the horse came down the hill A over T to crash to a halt in a dusty pile right at the marshal's feet.

An ordinary person would have been killed. But my new character jumped up laughing, and a pint bottle fell out of one of his back pockets. He was built like a wedge, with flaring wide ears, carrot-colored hair, and an alarming gap in his face where two of his front teeth should have been. He had a big Colt strapped on, and a stick of dynamite in the top of one of his boots. Nobody had ever been like this guy.

After getting over my inbred English department embarrassment at having created such an exaggeration, I found myself chuckling at this weirdo. He started talking, and he was totally outrageous. My interest in him—and the novel— soared. It was a struggle the rest of the way to prevent his taking over the story entirely.

I was still working as a student with Dwight V. Swain when this happened. I took pages of the novel to him for critique. I can still see him sitting up straighter behind his desk when my new character appeared, then beginning to read more intently, then starting to chuckle.

"Bickham," he chortled, slapping the pages with the back of his hand, "this is great. This is crude. Great barnbrush strokes. This *works*. We may get you over your experiences in the English department yet!"

That novel sold. My character still fascinated me. I decided to try a comic western starring him. When that one* was submitted, Tom Dardis at Berkley Medallion wrote to accept the book for publication, and suggested a series about him!

That was how Wildcat O'Shea was born, and eventually he starred in fourteen novels. I still remember him with great fondness. No, he was not great literature. But he brought me, and a lot of readers, fun and pleasure.

And he taught me that the key to characterization is exaggeration, not only for the reader but as a goad to the writer's imagination.

Try it!

What else is a character? How do we make up good ones?

Some of the process is mysterious, like the formation of initial story ideas, and I don't care to question it. We observe real people, have emotional reactions to them, think about them, live with them, and mix them together in our imagination to come up with composites and extensions. A lot of it simply happens for the creative person.

There are, however, a number of techniques and observations we can make to boost the process along. Let's try it again: what is a character in fiction?

A character is *a name*.

Sometimes we tend to grab a name for a major character out of the air, and fail to give it sufficient thought. But the name is sometimes the first way we begin to sense something about a character, and it's the single identity tag by which we will refer to her again and again and again. It's important.

---

*The Fighting Buckaroo by Jeff Clinton.

What if we call our character Mary Smith?

What if we change her name to Bubbles LaRue?

Or Fifi?

Or Sister Innocence?

Is there a difference implied only in the name between male characters called Dirk Pitt and Percy Dovetonsils? Between George Washington Jones and Tony DiRosario?

The name itself may suggest character type, history, even ethnic background. So it's important to find the right one as your work proceeds on building the character in your mind.

Will you refer to the character by full name, first name, or last name? The custom today is to refer to males by last name, females by first name, on second and subsequent reference. But it's by no means a universal. Referring to our character John Jones as "John" on subsequent reference tends to warm the tone of the story, subtly soften the style. "Jones" is cooler, but in some cases (especially in his viewpoint) may be too cool in some types of novels. Mary Smith will almost always be called "Mary" on later reference in viewpoint, even in this time of sexual equality. "Smith" often sounds just too cold. (This may be changing.)

In a spy novel or suspense yarn, where the tone is generally cool anyway, characters almost always will be called by their last names only. In a romance, where the tone is intimate, the opposite might be true. But it's a fact that changing your method of reference to a character in this small way may alter the tone of your entire passage. This also shows how important the character name may be.

A character is also *a personal history*.

How elaborately you devise the past for a character will depend, of course, on her role in the novel. It will also depend, to a lesser degree, on the type of story you plan to tell. In any case, however, for a major character you should at least be able to fill out an imaginary job application. The minimum information should include:

Name
Date and place of birth
Parents' names, ages, occupations, social status, and present whereabouts
Education
Marital status and children, if any
Military background, if any
Health
Job background
Financial situation
Awards, achievements of note, etc.
Ambitions
Hobbies and pastimes (possibly including favorite music, authors, sporting events, and entertainment personalities)

I have a form in my computer for this data on characters. You may wish to devise one of your own. Some of the information may never enter the story directly. But forcing your imagination to build such a background for your character will stimulate further thought and bring out new ideas about him —and much of the information may enter the novel indirectly, in ways that surprise you. For the better you know your character, the clearer you will inevitably depict him.

In addition, as has been implied before, a character is very importantly *a goal*. Someone once said, "Tell me what a person strives for, and I'll tell you the kind of person he is." Your study of the character's past, and how it leads to his present goal in the story, is vital.

The goal stems from, and relates to, the *self-concept*, another vital aspect of character. We talked about this at length in an earlier chapter. You may wish to refer back to that section to refresh your memory and consider the material strictly in the context of characterization.

To review briefly, here, however, let me just remind you

that our most central goal is maintenance and enhancement of the symbolic self, or self-concept. Out of your character's background and present situation has come a view of herself which is consistent and precious to her. Somehow her story goal relates to that self-concept; the role she plays in her life and the novel does, too. For every character who plays any significant role in your novel, you should have a sheet of paper, or a computer file, which contains her statement: "I am _____," using your imagination to fill out her self-definition in a few words.

Having done this, you can clarify your thinking about the roles she plays not only in the story, but in the rest of her life.

As an example, one woman may say:

I am a businesswoman, and very efficient in what I do.

Her roles, therefore, may include working for a major oil company; writing a book about better ways to use employees efficiently; dating a man whose work as an attorney she admires for its intelligence and power; driving a sleek British sedan because she admires the traditional British character; wearing business suits and practical shoes (but with higher heels and coolly feminine styles in the evenings), and living in a Manhattan apartment used by upwardly mobile professional people.

Another character, a man, may say:

I am an outdoorsman and an athlete.

Aside from the fact that he works for the Forestry Service, wears flannel shirts and drives a Bronco, I'll let you imagine how his entire environment is structured around roles that enhance his stated self-image.

Note also, however, that a character may often act the way he does not only out of a positive self-concept, but out of a negative one. By the process of accommodation, people often build a strength over what was once perceived as a weakness —real or imagined. How often have you seen a great athlete on TV in, say, the Olympics, and then heard the announcer tell how that marathon runner suffered polio as a child? How many fine public speakers once were terrified to face an audience, or even suffered a stutter or lisp? So sometimes a key to better understanding a character is to look for the lacking or old weakness that lies behind today's strength.

Examples abound of characters fighting to overcome old flaws they beheld in themselves as part of their self-concept— learning to play roles exactly the opposite of the weakness. In our recent history one need look no farther than a cripple who became a great president (despite being confined to a wheelchair), a wonderful jazz/popular pianist and vocalist who is blind, an NBA basketball player a full two feet shorter than many of his opponents. Find your character's hidden feeling of loss, weakness, vulnerability, and you may often find a key to his strength and dedication in your novel.

Self-definition thus becomes a cornerstone of characterization. As you become more aware of people in your everyday life, you will begin to hear them stating their self-concept in obvious ways that may have missed your attention up until now. Note all the ways people tell you who they think they are. You will be amazed to notice how consistent they are in being exactly the person they define.

Your journal should start to be sprinkled with specifics in this area.

A story character, however, is many other things too. He is also very importantly *a collection of tags and traits*.

Personality traits in the broadest sense are those rather abstract descriptors of personality that you can name but seldom explain. A man is strong, you say, or sympathetic, or nervous or overbearing.

Abstract words. Unconvincing. They paint no picture for the reader. And readers seldom believe what we as writers tell them; they want to be shown, and then allowed to draw their own conclusions about the story people, just as they observe people in real life and then draw conclusions about them.

So it is not enough for you, the author, to know that Joe is nervous, compulsive, impatient, and a little self-destructive. You have to devise a way to show these inner traits to the reader.

How? You hang tags on him.

A tag is simply an outwardly visible (or audible) appearance, activity, habit, or thing that you hang on the character, like a tag hanging on a piece of furniture, which says what the inner, abstractly named trait is.

Of course sometimes a tag is strictly a shorthand device to help the reader recognize a minor character, and this kind of tag may have little to do with personality. Your minor figure who works where the hero banks, for example, may wear pince-nez glasses and have a toupee that sometimes slips toward one ear. Or the mailman may limp, so that when we hear someone limp onto the porch we know who it is. Major tags for major characters, on the other hand, not only identify people in this way; they show something of what the person is like.

A personality tag is waved more often during the course of a novel than you might suspect. Readers forget. If, for example, you decide that one tag for "nervous Joe," mentioned just above, is that he smokes heavily, then in a 60,000-word novel you will probably show him smoking twenty or thirty times. In addition, you will devise *tag clusters* which all relate to his nervous smoking habit. You may show him asking for a light on four widely separated occasions, coughing six times, buying cigarettes twice, filling his lighter twice, opening a fresh pack three times, emptying an ashtray once, waving a hand with tobacco-stained fingers three or four times, and so on.

It may be that you will finally decide, on revision, that you waved a tag or tag cluster too often. You can always go back and delete a few. In my experience with new novelists, the opposite problem usually obtains: a good tag may be chosen, but then is wasted because it isn't shown nearly often enough. Good writers wave the tags often. How many times did Herman Wouk have Captain Queeg roll those steel balls around in his hand?* How many times did Hamlet express his indecisive nature in speech and action? How often did Spock tell Captain Kirk, "It isn't logical," or some variation that told of his non-emotional, Vulcan background?

Do you think tags don't affect your identification and perception of real-life people? See if you can identify anybody in the following list of tags:

"Let me make this perfectly clear. I am not a crook."

A cigar, a round face, a bald head, a V-for-victory sign

A singer wearing a glove on only one hand

"Wow! Did you see him come in and boom! make that tackle?"

A mustache; a strut; a stiff-armed salute, *"Heil!"*

A tennis player getting a bad line call and going berserk, arguing, breaking his racket, forfeiting the match

(For those who had trouble, the answers are below.)†

As an exercise, let me suggest that you thinly create as many as three or four new characters and devise tags to illustrate some of their more salient traits. If this takes a few hours or a couple of days, fine.

In the next chapter we'll look at a number of other aspects of

---

*The Caine Mutiny by Herman Wouk.

†In order: Richard Nixon; Winston Churchill; Michael Jackson; John Madden; Adolf Hitler; John McEnroe.

building fictional character. At this point, however, it's time to think a bit about how characters enter a story and conduct themselves inside it. Or to put it another way, how do we introduce a new person into the story, and how do we keep him identifiable?

The single most important moment for a major character may well be when he first enters the story. Therefore it is vitally important to bring your majors on in the proper way. A weak or wrong first impression on the reader may never be remedied.

How do we introduce or bring on characters? Through one of the following methods:

By characteristic entry action
By description of habitat
By other character comment
By direct author intrusion

Characteristic entry action is the most dramatic and most-used method. The door opens and in comes Marybell, doing and saying and acting and feeling and being absolutely characteristic. With all her tags waving. She makes an instant and lasting impression. The reader feels he begins to know her at once.

For example, Marybell comes into your office. She keeps her eyes lowered, she sort of glides apologetically, she sits with legs straight and tight together and nervously smoothes her plain cotton dress down over her knees; you notice she wears no polish on her bitten fingernails, and there is a little tic on the left side of her pale face, devoid of makeup.

The next day, here comes the new, redesigned, customized, jet-propelled Marybell, the model for the 1990s. She knocks briskly and swings into the office, electric with energy, swinging a tiny purse, her heels clicking sharply on the tiles. Her head is high, her hairdo is beautiful, she gives you a wide, confident grin and leans across your desk to shake hands, plumps down in the proffered chair, crosses pretty legs, whips out a notebook and ballpoint, and fixes you with those keen, intelligent blue eyes that stare with total confidence out of a perfectly made-up face.

Sometimes your plans for plot in a novel will be subtly altered because—in order to bring on your character in characteristic action—you have to put in a scene that will have few downstream effects. In other words, sometimes you plot for character. So maybe you have to put Jimmy the Pilot in an airline emergency to introduce him in a way that will show his daring, coolness, and resourcefulness. Or possibly you have to show Jennifer talking long-distance to her aged mother, to introduce her in an action that best demonstrates her characteristic kindness and devotion to her family.

Stop now. Think about your major character. If you could first introduce him onstage anywhere, at any time, to give him a smashing entrance:

Where would you have him?
What would he be doing?
How?
What tags would be waving?
What would be his overwhelming dominant impression?

Write it!

Characteristic entry action is a great way to bring on a character.

There are, of course, a few problems.

For one thing, you as a writer face the task of naming, identifying, and describing the new character at the same time she is talking and acting, at the same time another character is reacting, at the same time you're trying to keep plot moving, at the same time Marybell is coming on like gangbusters, at the same time—well, you get the idea. Introducing characters this way is hard because so much tends to happen all at once.

Another problem is that the reader might catch on to the trick if you do it for all the other characters. And you could end up with so much action for plot that you would be on page 80 before the real story got much of a start.

There are other ways, as we said.

Introduction by habitat is a technique once much-favored and done well by Harold Robbins. Here, before the character enters the scene directly, the author describes the character's office, or car, or apartment, or clothes closet, or country club —whatever may tell the reader about the roles the character plays, the kind of environment he has chosen or built around himself to enhance his self-concept—the habitat that says, indirectly, who and what he is.

An example off the top of my head:

> The office on the top floor of the forty-story bank building reeked of power. Its glass wall looked out over the heart of the financial district. Heavy carpet masked sounds of work beyond the closed walnut door. On one interior wall: shelves of books that included works on finance as well as great literature. Another wall was dominated by a small but priceless Picasso. The great walnut desk was clean, efficient, graced by a marble pen-and-pencil set and a framed picture of Harrigan himself with his beautiful young wife and their two children, whom he adored. Hidden in the bottom drawer on the righthand side of the desk was a booklet he had ordered and received only recently; it described many ways by which a man who was terminally ill might take his own life.

After such a static description of habitat—which might extend considerably longer than this little sample—we can have character Harrigan enter the habitat. And we already know a great deal about him.

Another method of character introduction is *comment by other characters*.

Here you simply set up a scene in which one character already introduced wants to know about the character you plan to bring on next. Use Harrigan as an example again, and suppose we know nothing about him. Have Don and Dave meet somewhere. Don says, "Harrigan is due to arrive today." Dave says, "I don't know a thing about him. What can you tell me?" Then the two have a conversation in which one character asks questions, and the other tells what you the author want the reader to know.

Having accomplished this method of introducing data to the reader, almost the way the ancient Greek theater chorus worked by commenting on the action for the audience, you can bring Harrigan onstage to a reader well prepared for his arrival.

Finally, you may sometimes introduce a character by *direct author intrusion*. One novelist who uses this technique a lot is Sidney Sheldon. The writer begins a new segment of his story by simply dumping in factual data about the new character. Or he may vary this approach slightly by writing a personality description that is close in style and intent to the old Greek "characters." Authors such as Theophrastus had a book of descriptions of characters by *type*—the glutton, the coward, and so forth.*

In your reading, try to be more alert as to how characters are brought on. Note how good novelists use one device one time, another the next. Variety of approach enlivens the narrative, and as you grow as a novelist, you'll see that one approach may fit one character better than another—and that how you bring your people on will also affect your pace in the book.

Beyond this, and before we begin to look deeper into human personality and character development in the next chapter, a few additional points need to be remembered.

Conflict creates character. There is nothing like the pres-

The Characters of Theophrastus by J. M. Edmonds, ed.

sure of a struggle—and the setbacks of scene endings—to bring out the true nature of your story person. Anyone can look good, or dull, when there is no pressure.

Whenever you are having trouble with a character, it may well be that you are not making life difficult enough for her.

Character is defined by action.

The internal life of a character may often be defined in large part through the judicious use of the *internalizations* that are an integral part of stimulus-response transactions. Make the stimulus-response transaction complex by making the stimulus tough or unexpected, and your character will be driven into a little sequel internalization before being able to respond. This will allow you to show how he thinks and feels.

Other characters define other characters. If you have set up a sympathetic character named Archibald, and he tells someone else that he would go to the wall for Biff, "a really great guy," then the reader will tend to believe Biff is a great guy before ever meeting him. In fiction, good people tend to like good people, and bad tend to like bad, and never the twain shall meet—except in conflict. Don't hesitate to let your story people characterize one another in conversation with each other.

Given half a chance, *your character will tell the world the kind of person he is.* As we discussed earlier, people in real life, and in fiction, often explain their behavior by saying, "I didn't steal the money because I'm an honest man." Or, "I can't spend the night, Jack, because I'm not that kind of girl." Or, "Basically, I'm a sentimental jerk, but at least I'm honest."

Don't be afraid to have your characters talk about themselves in this way. And please also note that sometimes you can create scenes in which two characters argue about one's view of the other—or about one's view of himself!

I don't think I'll elaborate on that. But I hope you think about it. It's a very useful device, and one very much in tune with the reality of how we function in real life.

In closing, let me suggest that you go back through this

chapter and follow up on some of the exercises implied in the discussion.

Name some characters and write backgrounds for them.

Devise some traits, and tags to match. Devise tag clusters.

Write a major background statement for at least one major character.

Write job-application forms for at least two others.

Take one of these characters and practice bringing her on in characteristic entry action. Through habitat. Through the other devices mentioned. See which works the best for you, and why.

Finally, chew on this one for a while: *Every major character has a characteristic preoccupation.* It has to do with background, felt needs and perceived lackings in the self-concept, story goal—virtually everything we've discussed.

What is your major character's characteristic preoccupation? To what worry, goal, sadness, or hope does she tend to relate almost anything she encounters?

Take your time on all this! If you press on before giving considerable time and thought to these matters, you're cheating yourself again.

Take a week at least.

When you don't have anything else to do and start feeling impatient, sit down in an easy chair, relax, and think about the color green.

11

....

Making Your Characters More Complex

*Real people often act
out of motives they don't understand.
The novelist must know
the reasons,
even if the characters don't.*

A basic understanding of some aspects of personality is a prerequisite for the writing of any novel that aspires beyond the most mechanical level.

Some people understand those around them with a compassion, sensitivity and insight that comes from the nature of their basic personality. Others of us have to study people—consciously in real life and through self-analysis and readings in psychology—in order to grope toward understanding of what makes others tick.

If you are one of those rare blessed ones who understands people almost at the level of instinct, I congratulate you. This chapter may offer very little that you don't already know. If, on the other hand, you are one of the vast majority, perhaps something here can help you make your story characters appear more realistic, which is to say, more complex.

Real people—and the best characters in fiction—often act out of motives they understand vaguely, if at all. "That's just the way I am," they say, inadvertently referring to their self-concept. Or, "I've always been that way, it's my basic temperament." This refers to an entire school of psychology that looks—not at *nurture,* as most psychology has tended to do since the time of Sigmund Freud—but at *nature,* traits of personality which may be programmed into the gene structure itself in ways we don't understand (or perhaps dictated in part by the uterine environment). Others may say, "I act this way because my family has always acted this way," perhaps preconsciously sensing the truths of Transactional Analysis and its emphasis on often-unexamined life scripts derived from parents, other family, or even from cultural/ethnic/national sources.

None of us can ever hope to understand it all. But the novelist can pick and choose, and out of even a superficial study can come up with an eclectic approach to the understanding of human behavior that will help enormously in making his story people more complex.

In your novel, the characters may not always show their true feelings because they don't know them, or because they can't face them, or because they're afraid to reveal them, or because they are dishonest.

The dishonest character in your book, in the broadest sense, does not necessarily have to be an unlikable person. Travis McGee, in the late John D. MacDonald's series, was often dishonest in that he withheld information from people for good reasons, or acted less intelligent and aware than he really was in order to defend himself. McGee especially loved to play the innocent oaf with police, throwing them off the track so that they ignored him and thus left him alone to pursue his investigations. James Bond seldom was entirely honest, as witness his classic deception of Goldfinger, tricking him into a high-stakes golf game.* (That sequence, incidentally, is also a classic lesson in pure scene structure.)

Beyond such characters as these and others who lie or deceive—and know they are doing it—there are many more who deceive themselves as well as everyone else. That's because they simply cannot face their basic feelings.

Such characters, and people in real life, often display one or more of four basic behaviors which are most useful to the novelist. They're fairly easily understood on a mechanical level, and give us a place to start.

These four puzzling behaviors have been observed by all of us at one time or another. They are: *projection, denial, reaction, and displacement.*

Let's look at them.

■ ■ PROJECTION ■ ■

In this behavior, the person may be aware of some of his feelings, but views his world unrealistically—and consequently acts dishonestly—because he projects his feelings onto others. His basic, unexamined assumption is, "All people feel as I do."

So the man with envy and thievery in his heart will assume that everyone else is the same, and will trust no one. He's likely to misconstrue the simplest well-meaning gesture as a maneuver to cheat or get him. Perhaps he'll have an elaborate burglar alarm system.

In romance, the woman madly in love with a man—even if he has shown no deep interest in her—may project her love onto him and truly believe he loves her as much as she loves

---

*Goldfinger by Ian Fleming.

him. Obviously, such a process sets her up for the most bitter and profound disappointment, and the man may or may not have done anything to encourage her delusions.

I once encountered a classic case of projection in real life. (Over the years I've witnessed many, just as you have.) It was a beautiful spring day and I happened to meet a female acquaintance on Main Street.

"Good morning!" I said. "Beautiful day, isn't it?"

"How can you say that?" she cried. "You don't have to pretend for *me*." And she burst into tears.

Later I learned she had just lost someone very dear to her. So *her* day was not beautiful, as we met on the street; she had projected her misery onto the entire environment. And when I said it was a pretty day, she immediately assumed I was pretending *because she was pretending* a calm she in no way really felt.

In engineering distrust, or setting up transactions between characters with a potential for disaster based on misunderstanding, you may find projection to be a useful device.

▪▪ DENIAL ▪▪

The process of denial, unfortunately, is one very, very common in real life. The person in denial represses totally whatever feelings may be down in there somewhere.

Taught that anger is unacceptable to his parents, for example, a male child may be faced with an intolerable conflict between his emotions and the demands of his parents, whom he loves. His feeling and showing of anger results in condemnation or rejection by his parents, or punishment. He learns quickly to feel bad about himself—his sense of self-worth suffers—when anger swells up inside him. So without conscious volition he learns a trick: to bury such unacceptable feelings and not allow them at all into his consciousness.

In one sense, this results in what we mean when we speak of "the unconscious." Part of this portion of one's personality is composed of feelings and thoughts that are simply too terrible (in reality or imagination) to be allowed into consciousness. They are still there, but we bury them—literally no longer know they exist.

And so our angry child grows up to become a man who can quite honestly (as far as he knows!) tell you: "I simply don't ever get angry. Anger is an emotion I never experience." The young female, sensing potential rejection by her mother for experiencing the most innocent sexual stirrings, denies all such feelings—and grows up to be a cold and frigid wife. Or the youth denied love, ridiculed as a sissy for showing love, or given no good examples in how to demonstrate love, may become an adult who feels no love for anyone and borders on the behavior patterns of the sociopath.

Use of denial in characters is often helpful to the novelist. If the denying character is placed in plot circumstances wherein the denial is tested again and again—and finally broken through—enormous amounts of energy may be liberated, and a character's life can be thrown into tumultuous upheaval as if at the click of a switch.

▪▪ REACTION ▪▪

On the day John F. Kennedy was shot in Dallas, I was working in a newspaper office in Oklahoma City. The newsroom, after the chaotic rush to get out a special edition detailing the tragedy, was silent as a tomb. Across the room from me somewhere was Janis, a woman reporter who, I knew, had revered the fallen president.

Suddenly, I heard loud laughter across the big room. Turning in shock, I saw that it had come from Janis. I was horrified, and it was much later that I finally realized she had been in reaction without, of course, any awareness of what she was doing.

In her extreme grief, she had suddenly started reacting against her painful feelings by acting just the opposite.

Why? Perhaps in this case she simply could not fully face her pain. But the protection of simple denial failed her. The feelings broke through and were there, overwhelming in their intensity. And so she turned to her next line of psychological defense, a reaction that showed her acting out the precise opposite of what she was really feeling, almost as if by pretending to be happy, she might be.

Irrational? Of course. But there are parts of us, as we shall see, that have nothing to do with rationality or logic. And we live with them, too. Sometimes when the pressure is the greatest, rationality breaks down and these more primitive modalities of survival break to the surface, ruling us.

You may quickly think of many cases in which you have witnessed, or even taken part in, reaction. The urge to giggle during a solemn portion of a religious service; the burst of anger out of sadness, when you really feel so defenseless and weak; a rush of bitter invective toward a lover when your heart is breaking and you are on the brink of tearful collapse.

In your novel, the shy, frightened girl might suddenly begin acting like a whore, or the equally scared man might strut like a Don Juan. They—and the characters surrounding them— might be puzzled or shocked by their behavior. But you will understand the process driving them, and readers will recognize the truthfulness of your characterization on an instinctive level, even if they don't have the first word to describe what they recognize in the gut.

▪▪ DISPLACEMENT ▪▪

Displacement behavior is one of the most interesting and useful patterns for the writer of fiction. Here, as in the other syndromes mentioned, the character is trying unconsciously to protect herself from facing feelings that are simply not acceptable. But in this case, the feeling or impulse is expressed—but in a disguised way, or aimed in the wrong direction.

Examples. When my children were young, I often noticed that arguments broke out among them when I told them it was time to pick up the toys in the living room and go to bed. Invariably Bobby accused Danny of making the toy mess, Danny said it was Stephen's fault, Stephen yelled at Lise to do her share before he hit her. Lise, in her turn, would more than likely yell back at one of them.

What was happening? They didn't want to pick up the room. They didn't want to have to go to bed. They were angry at *me;* but attacking me was unacceptable behavior. So they displaced their anger and argument to one another.

Once in a novel I had a hero, highly frustrated by the heroine, have a scene with her in the fenced backyard of a house. He argued and pleaded and she was sniffy, cold and thoroughly irritating. My hero got madder and madder and more and more frustrated until he was clearly about to explode. Finally, when she said something ultimately insulting and maddening, he balled his fists, trembled from head to foot, turned, and *attacked the board fence*.

Consider another example. A young woman yearns for family love and closeness, but is denied. She enters a religious order and becomes "a bride of Christ." This is not to suggest that all or even very many nuns enter the convent for reasons anything like this, but it's possible. In such a case, the impulse toward family, possible marriage, and sexuality are, for whatever reason, not acceptable. So the impulse is directed into another sector—the religious life. Classic displacement.

You may frequently find occasions in your novels where the character would be too obvious or predictable if she showed exactly what was on her mind. A villainous character, especially, may need to make moves that are baffling and confusing to everyone, the reader included. You may wish to consider the psychology of that character in terms of displacement. Maybe he doesn't really mean to attack our hero at all; maybe he's mad at his wife—and he can't attack her, so he attacks elsewhere.

The psychology section of your favorite bookstore is sure to contain dozens of books that include descriptions of other behaviors, which you might find equally interesting or useful. These are all, to some degree, neurotic behavior patterns. But they are as common as apple pie. Use them in good health. They'll help you complicate your major characters, and because they are so common, readers will see and understand them easily enough, without serious prejudice against the character so afflicted.

A note of warning, however: some of the books you may encounter will go into clinical detail about behaviors much more serious than the ones we've mentioned. When you study these psychoses, and try to put them into your stories, you're getting into very deep water indeed, and run a much greater risk of losing or alienating your readership.

A little craziness, in other words, is "normal" enough! Too much is . . . well . . . too much.

■ ■ TRANSACTIONAL ANALYSIS AND ■ ■ LIFE SCRIPTS

Perhaps no area of contemporary psychology is as helpful to the novelist in deepening the motivation and humanity of her characters as Transactional Analysis. Again, let's look at some of this discipline's tenets so that you can pick and choose aspects that may help you, merging the TA view with whatever other psychological information you may also find helpful.

The discipline is so called because its founder, Dr. Eric Berne, observed in his psychiatric practice that clients related to one another in therapy groups in ways characteristic of their ways of relating in outside life. By analyzing group therapy transactions, Berne decided, he and group members could reveal, and analyze, clients' ways of functioning with other people.

This led to Berne's development of games theory, the idea that people functioning unhealthily with others often played games—repetitive, self-defeating procedures that made real human contact impossible, and "paid off" in bad feelings all around.*

While game analysis is an invaluable therapeutic tool, and very useful for the novelist who goes beyond the basics, the greatest value of Transactional Analysis is in the theory which Berne developed as an underpinning for his observations. We have all had the experience of being torn while trying to make a decision—almost as if we were hearing different voices inside our heads. The classical Freudian might think these differing impulses came from id, ego, or superego. The Christian traditionalist might think about the conscience as a source of one voice. Berne, however, proceeded a bit differently.

Berne put his focus on the ego, humankind's rational faculty, and, pragmatist that he was, thus eliminated mystery and mumbo jumbo. He then suggested that the human personality is divided into three ego states, the Parent, the Adult, and the Child. These ego states are universally drawn, for theoretical convenience's sake, as three circles:

---

*Games People Play by Eric Berne.

The *Parent ego state* is the seat of nurturing impulses, whether directed toward yourself or someone else. It may also express itself in critical comments of the kind that might be concluded with a statement such as, "I'm telling you this (or suggesting this) for your own good!"

The *Adult ego state* is a data processor, that part of our functioning we are in when we take in factual information and deal with it in an objective way. When you ask someone what time it is, and they tell you, it's an adult-to-adult transaction. The Adult also listens to internal dialogues between the Parent and the Child ego state.

The third ego state is *the Child*. The Child is the seat of emotion, creativity, willful impulses, manipulation—just about all those aspects of personality that make us appealing (or otherwise!)—and can often get us in trouble. When we really play, we are said to be "in our Child." So, too, it is the Child who loves, hates, laughs, sings, and weeps.

The goal of healthy functioning, according to Berne (and many who have followed him), is to be able to move from one ego state to another at will, depending on the situation and which ego state cathexis (energizing and putting in command) is appropriate. In a business meeting which begins with analysis of budget data, includes a lunch at which one provides loving sympathy for a worried employee, and concludes with a dance party, for example, it might be appropriate to be in the Adult for the data, the Parent for the lunch, and the Child (with the Adult hovering near for protection) during the party.

How is this theory useful to you as a novelist? In many ways.

Acceptance of the fundamentals of TA gives you another basis on which to found puzzling character behavior. Your female lead, for example, may show a lightning change from near-maternal concern to a foot-stamping outburst of childlike disappointment.

Even more interesting, what TA practitioners call the

crossed transaction is often a source of conflict. Earlier I mentioned a transaction that might go like this:

YOU: Pardon me, dear, but what time is it?
SHE: It's eight o'clock.
YOU: Thank you.
SHE: You're welcome.

Great! This is a harmonious exchange of information, an Adult-to-Adult transaction.

But what if it goes like this?

YOU: Pardon me, dear, but what time is it?
SHE: Damn, damn, damn! I'm so mad at you!
YOU: What did I do? What—
SHE: I'm sick of your asking me things! Don't you know I'm busy and tired? I just feel yuk!

Now a fight has started, perhaps, or at least there's an element of conflict, because the transactions have gotten crossed.

In the first example, you asked from your Adult and she replied from her Adult. This illustrates the principle that complimentary transactions, in which the ego state addressed is the one that replies, may proceed harmoniously (although not always). But when the transaction is crossed, as in the second example, trouble looms and conflict may go on virtually forever.

In the second transaction, you asked out of your Adult. She responded, with anger, out of her frustrated Child. This crossed the lines of communication, as shown below.

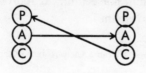

Confused, conflictful interchanges, TA theory suggests, may go on forever because nothing ever gets accomplished. Understanding of this principle allows the storyteller to create conflict out of the simplest transaction between story people, with resulting confusion and hard feelings. On another level of your awareness as a writer, it's always good to be aware of what ego state your people are in as they maneuver, worry, and square off.

Let me hasten to add that they don't have to be in different ego states for conflict to occur. Two people, gravely concerned about a third, might differ radically about the best way to parent the third party with help or advice—or by leaving the third person alone. There can be serious disagreements about how to analyze data, an Adult-Adult transaction. Both parties can be in their Child, one trying cleverly to manipulate, the other having a temper tantrum.

Often, when transactions get crossed, as you can readily see, game playing can take place. Berne's wonderful book on games defines classic, repetitive games, which always have a payoff in bad feelings. Fiction characters—like people in real life—can be observed again and again playing such common ones as "I Was Only Trying to Help," or "Why Don't You Yes But," or "Now I've Got You, You Son of a Bitch," or "Rapo." Other writers have discovered and defined other games.

In game playing, as suggested by a later TA theorist, players usually enter a "drama triangle."* The drama triangle can be drawn as follows:

Where P stands for "persecutor," R represents the "rescuer" role, and V means "victim."

---

*"Fairy Tales and Script Drama Analysis" by S. Karpman.

Once sucked into the drama triangle, you or your character will find baffling, maddening, and wholly frustrating things going on.

Suppose, for example, Dad walks in to find son Billy making a mess in the kitchen while Mom is in the utility room. Dad bawls out Billy, and Billy starts to bawl. Dad is the persecutor and Billy is the victim. Dad is also rescuing Mom. Then Mom runs into the room and plays rescuer to Billy's victim by becoming persecutor to Dad, saying, "What have you done to the poor child now?" Dad, now in the victim role, starts to sulk, and leaves the room, muttering, "I was Only Trying to Help." (His favorite game.) At which point Mom sees the mess Billy was making, starts screaming at him (Now I've Got You, You Son of a Bitch) from a persecutor role, Billy yells that she should have stayed out of it (persecutor, making her the victim playing another common game, Poor Me), and so on. Everyone is baffled, everyone is unhappy, everyone is playing games —and the poles can switch with lightning speed so that nobody knows what in the hell is going on here.

(The only way to stay out of the drama triangle in real life, incidentally, is to recognize invitations, and not play. Games players will hate you for it, and immediately see you as a persecutor to their victim. That's their problem.)

There is a world of wonderful information useful to the writer—both as a writer and in her own day-to-day functioning—available in the literature of Transactional Analysis. TA practitioners and theorists have an international organization and magazine. The temptation is to press on here with details of divisions within the Child, second-order analysis, functional analysis, and more. But the above should get you started on this aspect of TA if you are sufficiently motivated.

One more aspect of TA must be discussed, however, because it is so invaluable in building character background. That is the concept of *life script*.

According to Berne's theory, exquisitely amplified by

Claude M. Steiner,* among others, people very early in their lives, and without realizing it, draw conclusions about reality and the people around them, and mentally write a script for the way their life is going to be.

Messages of two kinds come to a small child from parents and significant others. Some of these are positive moral precepts and advice, which flow from the Parent of the parents to the little one. Called *drivers,* they include such things as "Work hard," "Be perfect," "Try, try again," and the like. These are usually given verbally, and grownups will often be heard repeating family drivers as if they were gospel.

At the same time, however, negative feelings and attitudes may flow nonverbally from the Child of the parents to the little one. These are called *injunctions*. The message may be very lethal. Common ones include "Don't grow up," "Don't feel," "Don't be important," "Don't make it," and, the most lethal of all, "Don't be."

Sometimes, good-sounding drivers automatically carry along a near-lethal injunction. The little one, urged to try to be perfect, will never succeed; the task is impossible. So the person with a "Be perfect" driver will always carry along as well a "Don't make it" injunction.

Taking in the drivers and injunctions and making decisions on the basis of childhood wisdom, the person forms her life script; seldom is she aware of its implications. She goes through life making crucial decisions just as if she really were carrying a printed script in her hands.

For the novelist, devising pictures of the character's early home life—the drivers and injunctions and the resulting character script—is an amazingly useful tool. Script matrix analysis is considered in many TA books, some of which you have already encountered in the footnotes. I want to encourage you as strongly as I can to follow up on these few suggestive com-

---

Scripts People Live by Claude M. Steiner.

ments, and arm yourself with this potent characterization arsenal.

There are, of course, all manner of other psychological ideas and constructs that might be mentioned here. You may already have found some of them. I urge you to further your study as much as time allows. It's a fascinating and fruitful area for the novelist, who has a large enough canvas to portray character in depth.

The study of human personality and characterization is a lifelong quest. And a fascinating one. The only requirements are courage to face oneself and compassion.

12

....

Other Problems

Q. "What about flashback?"
A: "Worry about things that are important, okay?"

Developing novelists worry about the damnedest things.

Flashback, for example.

This dialogue (quoted above) inevitably takes place at some time during nearly all of my writing courses. When the student writer gets my response, she often shows dismay and shock.

Flashback is an overrated device. And its use—the when and the how—has already been explained adequately, by implication, in the chapter on scene and sequel. Flashback is simply an author intervention or a part of a sequel in which past events are played back onstage moment by moment, as if they were now, to clarify present events and character motives. Flashback is never shoveled into the narrative for its own sake.

Flashback—as opposed to review of old events in summary

—will happen when story demands, or not. If you never write a flashback, don't worry about it. It's not something you have to have in there, like air in your tires.

What you do have to have in your novel are two other ingredients: *backstory* and *hidden story*.

Backstory is the history of events that took place before your novel began on page one. Hidden story is action that is taking place offstage, while your presented scenes are being played for the reader.

In some novels, backstory may be relatively unimportant. But in a novel where actions far in the past finally come out to influence present events—as in, say, a case of mistaken identity, a hidden inheritance from a generation past, or a very old crime—the backstory may have to be plotted in considerable detail just so you as author will know what old secrets and hidden motives lie behind the present action.

In a recent novel of mine, for example, the story begins in the present time and plays for five present days. But in order to set everything up as I wanted it, I had to start plotting the backstory—very little of which was ever told in the novel—in 1928.

If your story is of the type that requires considerable, detailed backstory plotting, do it carefully and well. Check your dates and chronology. Once one of my books inadvertently got as far as copyediting with a backstory whose unexamined chronology had my hero fathering a child at age eleven! (God bless copyeditors.)

There are two temptations about backstory you must learn to resist. One is to dump it all into the present narrative just because you know it's there. The other is to get so enamored of backstory that you spend too much time plotting previous generations when it isn't necessary.

Hidden story is often more necessary in terms of your loving attention, and can be both fun and maddening to plan. In timing your plot by cause and effect, it's always mandatory to figure out what your villain, for example, is doing while the hero is onstage. If you want the antagonist to burst onto the scene at

4:05 P.M., in Cleveland, you may have to plan (while he isn't
showing at all in the hero's viewpoint) that he decided the day
before at 7 P.M. to go to Cleveland (which may require you to
plot an unplayed scene or scenes and sequels to lead him to
this decision). Then that he bought a ticket at 10 A.M. today,
that he went to the airport at noon (which is why, perhaps,
someone else onstage got no answer from his telephone at that
hour, enhancing the mystery and worry about his whereabouts), that his plane was late, that he arrived in Cleveland at
2:30, that he got a taxi at 3:00, and so on.

▪▪ DIALOGUE ▪▪

Remember that few of your characters are onstage in view of
the audience at any given time. But all those others are back-
stage somewhere, and they're still living their lives and making
their plans which you must know if they are to reappear at the
right times in the right (that is, most complicating) places.

When characters do appear onstage, chances are that they
will be in dialogue. Dialogue is the lifeblood of most contemporary scene. We discussed earlier how dialogue must follow
the patterns of stimulus and response, and how dialogue paragraphs are formed. To refresh your memory, let's review the
principles we mentioned at that time.

Simplify your dialogue transactions. Send one tennis ball
over the net at a time. If a character wants to ask what time it
is, mention that it's a nice day, and say he is leaving at mid-
night for London, you must break up this information so that
he first only asks what time it is and gets an answer; says it's a
nice day and gets an answer; then says he is leaving for London, and gets an answer. (In each case, you can easily make up
a response for the other party which not only replies to his

stimulus, but in turn becomes a stimulus which partly causes him to enter his next step in the transaction.)

Paragraph dialogue elements together. The rule here is you have four things that happen in dialogue: the spoken words, the attribution, the stage action, and (possibly) introspection. However many you choose to have in a given stimulus or response package, they should all go in the same paragraph. When it's time for the other player to return the ball, you start a new paragraph.

The dialogue package item to which you want a response should go last in the paragraph. Thus if Joe says he's sorry and extends his hand, the other party will respond to his hand. But if he extends his hand and then says he's sorry, the other party will respond to his words.

There are a few dialogue devices which also should be mentioned beyond this review, which was put in with malice aforethought because so many people in my experience hear what was just said, but never really understand it.

The other ideas can be briefly stated as follows.

To link elements of dialogue, you might use one of the following devices:

Use *question and answer.* When one character is questioning another, and the second character is being at all responsive, the dialogue units link tightly.

Allow one character to interrupt the other. When Bart starts to say something and Karen breaks in, the link is tight and immediate, as in this example:

"As I was saying to my mother—"
"Do we always have to talk about her?"

Use *repetition of key words.* The characters in dialogue pick up on key words from one another, and their repetition syntactically ties the exchanges close.

Karen said, "I want a divorce."
"A divorce?" Bart choked. "I don't understand!"
"You never have understood."

"Never? I thought we understood each other so well!"

"Damn you! Can't you see what I'm saying?"

"All I can see is I love you—"

"Love?" Her expression was bitter. "You don't know what the word means."

Because he depended so heavily on dialogue, Ernest Hemingway's stories remain classic examples of brief, tight dialogue. So do Dashiell Hammett's. And, for that matter, F. Scott Fitzgerald's. Along with your study of current novels, you may profit from studying these masters.

You may also want to consider *body language* as a field of additional study as you look for facial expressions, gestures, bodily movements and postures which could be useful as stage action in dialogue interchanges. Some postures—arms crossed across the chest when the person is feeling defensive, for example—are so obvious as to be clear to most of us. Others are not as apparent.

A number of years ago, writer Julius Fast wrote a popular book entitled *Body Language*. A copy should be available in your library, and is worthy of study. Now that you know a smattering of Transactional Analysis, a much more detailed and scientific book may also be of interest. Author David A. Steere's book, *Bodily Expressions in Psychotherapy*, examines all sorts of hints—changes in posture and body alignment—which tip off otherwise hidden emotional reactions as well as the ego state a subject may be in at the time. This book, complete with many sketches of subjects, is a gold mine for the novelist looking for rich detail in the area.

Much of this brief chapter has presupposed something we discussed much earlier, and that is that each of us carries around with us a largely unexamined model of what a novel is *for us*. Part of our lifelong quest for excellence as writers should be examination of contemporary writers we admire, analysis of their techniques, and struggle to learn from them and grow surer in our execution of our own view of what a novel should be.

■■ A GAME PLAN ■■

For whatever it may be worth, I will share briefly with you a view of the architecture of a novel as I see it in the broadest general terms. It's a game plan, if you will, and it goes something like this in terms of how you proceed.

Establish a person in a setting with a problem.

The person must be exaggerated, traited, tagged, with a background sufficient to drive her, and she must be bothered greatly by some change in her universe which has upset her equilibrium, threatened her self-concept, and stirred her to fight.

Put this person onstage already in motion toward some specific shorter-term goal. The shorter-term goal relates to the long-term goal, which provides the umbrella story question the reader will worry about throughout the novel.

Establish an adversary—a person who will provide the primary source of conflict—as soon as possible.

Develop a sequence of scenes to bring in other characters and tighten the suspense. Others enter because they too have much to win or lose; they take sides. The picture becomes muddier.

Establish one or more subplots relating to the main plot. People these. Work on the background of these characters and their relationship to the hero and villain.

Move the hero (or villain) into his game plan of action.

Devise disasters to end scenes, propel the viewpoint character into sequels, and deepen the suspense. (Of course such setbacks also hook the reader.)

Alternate viewpoints in the body of the novel, but make sure that the primary viewpoint clearly dominates. There should be more scenes involving your number one character than any other, for example. And sometimes, when you're in other viewpoints, those people should be concerned about the fate of the major player.

Make sure the hero can't resign from the action. Tighten the ropes around him. Increase his desperation.

In the last third of the book, if at all possible, *set a ticking clock*. Perhaps it's as simple as one character saying to another, "I can't handle much more of this. I'm going to force a show-down Saturday night—twenty-four hours from now." Or it might be more sinister—a final ultimatum from rebellious convicts holding hostages, the deadline for payment of a ransom, or whatever.

Setting a ticking clock—a final day and time on which the reader knows the action must climax—heightens suspense greatly. In your reading, notice how often clocks are set.

Conclude with a decision in action which provides climax through sacrificial decision and reversal. Out of which will come payoff excitement—and revelation of theme.

Your own emerging vision of the ideal novel may be quite different from the simplified prototype just above. If it is, can you write it out in terms descriptive of how you approach your material to get your effects? If you can't yet, it's just one more thing to be working on in the weeks and months, and years, ahead.

One suggested assignment: write down an outline of the kind of novel you think is "yours." It may be vague, and may say in places things like, "Here she usually falls in love." Fine! Test to see how clear you really are about your own vision. Believe me, the exercise may pay dividends for you in ways you can at this moment scarcely imagine.

Finally, as you work on your novel, remember that your vision may change. Trust your feelings. Don't discount sound professional advice, but don't change things at random, to please everyone in your class or writer's club, either.

For ultimately it's your book, your baby. And that of your main character.

When you get most discouraged, do this:

Imagine your main character sitting in the chair across the empty room from you. Ask him or her how things seem to be going.

Cross the room physically, sit in the character's chair, stare back at yourself, imagined in the chair you just vacated, and reply.

Cross the room again, letting the physical movement back and forth contribute to the hypnotic role-playing.

You may learn new things about your story person—and the exercise can stimulate and refresh you.

Think it sounds crazy to be walking back and forth across an empty room, talking to a set of alternatingly empty chairs? Maybe so. It works. Try it.

13

·················

Revision and Submission

Careful revision
of manuscript
should be done
in thoughtful stages.

Good novels aren't written. They're rewritten and revised.

There are as many ways to block out and write a first draft as there are novelists around. Some writers meticulously outline every scene and sequel before writing actual text word one. Others scribble a few notes on an envelope, make up names for their characters (and everything else) as they go along, and simply plunge in. I recommend having at least a short synopsis of major plot developments and some calendar or clock notations to help remember what day it is, and what generally has to happen next.

Whatever method (or lack thereof) you use, however, at some point you're going to have a first draft, and the first draft is probably going to be a mess.

That's okay. I urge my students to write first drafts at white heat, never second-guessing themselves or looking back, dropping "fix notes" in the copy box if they must, but pressing on without getting hung up on small worries and problems. This prevents the writer from blocking or compulsively writing and rewriting the same segment over and over—and perhaps never getting an entire draft done. Once the pages of a first draft are in the box, they can always be fixed later.

Of course there are writers like Brian Garfield who say they never put a page of copy in the box until it's finished—as perfect as they can make it. And certainly no one can argue with Brian's success using this method. But I think most novelists, when they finish a draft, have also finished something of a mess. There are pages or computer files stacked atop one another along with notes of proposed changes, memos about problems and plants, and additional research data. Once I found this woeful notation on a student's chapter: change everything in this chapter!

How does one attack such a mess? There are as many ways to revise as there are to write the draft in the first place. A few observations—a working order—may be helpful.

First, you should go through the manuscript and do the repairs that have been in the back of your mind as you proceeded. If you changed the name of a character, for example, or altered your perceptions of one, if you changed assumptions about the time scheme of certain segments, or remembered later that a sequel needed to be inserted in Chapter 16—you go back and fix these things. Just interleave them or insert them in the computer file, and if the seams still show where you did the patch job, don't worry about that yet. Get the major patches and changes stuck in there in the right places.

Next draw up a new calendar and time scheme on which you jot major plot developments as they occur. Check your manuscript against this time plan to make sure you give Archie time to drive from Mansfield to Dallas, and don't have the grapevines pushing (blooming) in September when they do that in the spring. That sort of thing.

Having done that, you can begin *preliminary analysis*.

Here's a simplified checklist for this work, which you can do at your desk, turning pages, making marginal notes, writing new revision notes to yourself. There is no special significance to the order in which the checklist items are mentioned. You may start anywhere and work in any order—just as long as you get every item attended to.

■ ■ TIME SCHEME ■ ■

1. Is enough space allotted to pass sufficient reader time for believable transitions?

2. Are scenes developed properly, that is, moment by moment? (Look for inadvertent summary, which might spoil everything.)

3. Is there sequel-transition reader time between the really big scenes so they don't detract from one another by being bashed together back-to-back?

4. Does the manuscript need cutting, especially in the middle where stories tend to sag and lose momentum?

5. Does it need a new minor subplot to build up that sagging midsection?

6. Look at the climax. Often, drafts fall flat at the end because of writer fatigue. Does the climax come too fast, without sufficient buildup? Is it written for all it's worth?

7. Do major events occur in straight—often dull!—chronological order, or have you ordered them for maximum dramatic buildup?

8. Does the time factor tighten as the book proceeds?

9. Do your scenes and sequels follow logically, in stimulus-response fashion, even if the reader is sometimes surprised?

10. Is there a clock ticking? Could you set one?

11. Look at moments of big decision. Do characters seem to make these too swiftly, giving the reader the impression (by little reader time) that the decision was too easy or impulsive? Conversely, have you taken too much space (and time) for decisions anywhere, with resulting drag?

12. Check your time pointers. Is it always clear to the reader what day it is? What time? How, in time, this scene relates to the ones before and after it?

13. Check the timing of your hidden story. Make sure things offstage have time to happen, even if they don't play. Make sure things offstage are happening in the right order, in terms of stimulus-response, for whatever missiles come over the curtain to the forestage. (You can use different colored pencils to add this material to your calendar-planning sheet. I use black for onstage action, red for stuff that happens offstage, penciling both kinds of information into the same calendar blocks.)

■■ STORY LOGIC ■■

1. Is there reason for the major characters to want what they want? (Goes back to self-concept, script, background and backstory, but also to stimulus and response.)

2. Is it clear why they have selected their specific goals?

3. Do they have good reasons for going after their goals in the ways they do?

4. Check crucial setback points. Why doesn't the hero quit now? If only a madman (or a plot pawn shoved by the author) would go on here, you need to build up his motives.

5. Does coincidental good luck play a part in working things out? It shouldn't.

6. Search out all coincidence in the plot. You may have overlooked a lot. Use of coincidence—the chance meeting on the street, the lucky timing of a phone call—is almost always a sign of bad work and unconvincing story.

7. At all crucial turning points, are your solutions the most obvious? If so, they'll be outguessed by the reader, too. Search for other solutions and twists. Make lists to jog your imagination into fresher ideas.

■■ CHARACTER DEVELOPMENT ■■

1. Look at your major characters. Do we know enough background on all of them?

2. Are they colorful?

3. Reasonably attractive and interesting? (Characters don't have to have warts and runny noses to be realistic!)

4. Are they exaggerated?

5. Tagged?

6. Introduced forcefully?

7. Consistent but not boring?

8. Motivated and in action nearly all the time?

9. Do they have some hidden flaws?

10. Do you know their self-concept and something of their script?

11. Are they capable of surprising the reader?

12. Are they larger than life?

13. Do their problems in the outside plot world exacerbate whatever problems lurk within their hearts?

▪▪ SCENE STRUCTURE ▪▪

1. Examine all the big scenes. Are they truly big?
2. Can you see a way to build any of them even bigger?
3. Can you make scenes out of any possible chance encounters? Can that walk in the park be turned into a chase? Could you turn that casual conversation about the weather into a brief argument about wearing a coat?
4. Are there places where you let adversity play a role when you might build a scene around conflict instead?

▪▪ SUSPENSE AND SALESMANSHIP ▪▪

1. Look for the spots where that editor in New York is going to put this manuscript down and never pick it up again. What can you do to put hooks into those soft spots?
2. What's the angle—in plot, setting, or character—that may intrigue that New York editor because it's a little different or unusual? If you have none, can you put one in? If you have one, can you make it stronger?
3. Conversely, in your hasty, excited first drafting, are there places that are simply too wild and woolly, even—on sober reflection—bordering on the hysterical? Your cool professional judgment, not your fear, has to ferret these out if any are there. If you decide after reflection that something really is too much, now is the time to tone it down, take it out, or replace it.
4. Having done all this work, which may take many weeks if

done with sufficient care, I suggest that you reoutline the book as it now stands, including in the proper places any new segments you plan to add. This outline, in other words, represents what will be after rewrite. It should be bare bones plot summary—perhaps six to ten pages—and almost telegraphic.

5. With the book stripped down to this skeletal frame, look for flaws and holes. If you find some, patch them up with copy inserts.

6. Brood a bit. Be critical of the manuscript in a positive, professional way. Don't despair! Anything that's wrong, you can fix now.

7. Having done all this, you should interleave or insert all the new material you've come up with, and take out necessary cuts, again not worrying about the seams showing.

8. Then make chapter by chapter notes for any further structural or major character repairs you may be considering.

9. By this time, if things are going well, you have a manuscript that looks like an accordion that had a blowout. But the mess that was all over your desk (and floating around in your mind) is now a single, concentrated mess—a manuscript with all kinds of inserts and notes stuck in, and a couple of small outlines and plan sheets on top. You're getting there!

Now you're ready for *midstream analysis*. In the midstream, you're narrowing your focus to a few items you might have overlooked before.

■■ EXAMINE YOUR LANGUAGE AND ■■ SYNTAX

You're probably going to hate your style at this point. Don't worry about that. Look for repetitive words you may have overlooked. Check sentence length variety. (If you have a Grammatik or spellchecker in your computer, do not—repeat, do not—run it. These programs are fine, but we're talking about literary style and pacing here, not word count or computer nitpicking.)

■■ LOOK AT CHAPTER OPENINGS ■■

Do they always open after a major time transition? They shouldn't. You don't open or close chapters to provide seams where big time-gap transitions can be sneaked in. Sometimes the chapter should be an immediate continuation of the one that preceded it.

Do they always mark a change in viewpoint? They shouldn't. You're getting predictable if they do.

Do they always begin with dialogue?

With description?

With narration?

Vary your chapter openings in terms of scene-sequel structure, timing, and everything else.

■■ LOOK AT CHAPTER ENDINGS ■■

Most should end with scene disaster hooks. But not all.

Do they all end with dialogue? With internalization? With, "Now I lay me down to sleep"? Vary your endings just like your openings. Again please note: chapters were not invented so that you could drop troublesome time transitions into the white space that separates them.

▪▪ CHECK CHAPTER LENGTH ▪▪

Chapters should generally—stress generally—be of similar length. How long? Who cares? Ten to twenty pages? Fine. If you have an occasional chapter which dramatic pacing dictates be considerably shorter than the others, don't worry about it. You may worry that the book is ragged or uneven. But that's an author concern to be ignored. Readers don't notice "ragged;" readers notice dull.

Look for padding you put in to make a chapter long enough. Remove the padding!

Next comes what I call *late revision*. This is easy to describe. Using all your notes and fixes, start the actual rewrite. Work thoughtfully and steadily. Do at least a page or two every day to maintain pace and creative focus. Remember that writer pace is not story pace is not reader pace. Be patient. Don't get discouraged now!

Beware of "inspiration" at this point. Many novels have gone haywire because a tired novelist started off on some new wild trek that seemed more fun than what she already had on the page. At this point, lots of things may look better to you than what you already have on the page. That's fatigue talking. Don't listen. Follow your notes and plan.

Recognize the inevitability of fatigue, discouragement, distress, fear, and all that other good stuff that novelists live with in the late stages of a long project. Press on!

The final stage.

At some point, perhaps months after beginning your final rewrite, you will have a manuscript printed out and in the box. You're ready to rush it into the mail!

Not quite!

One or two more steps, please.

Put the box in your file drawer, and, for at least two weeks, work on something else or go to the beach or play records or catch up on movies or whatever you've probably been neglecting in the horrific press to finish the book. If you're a wife, you can even cook a real meal some night. If you're a husband, you can even cut the grass this week. Just don't do it so often your spouse gets overconfident!

This gives you a little time to let the manuscript cool. Your mind is off it just as much as possible.

When you go back to it, chances are that you still won't be able to see it as an outside reader might. In my experience, it takes more than a decade for a book really to cool out so I can read it like a stranger's work.

You can, however, get a scintilla of distance in just a couple of weeks, if you don't worry the project during the cooling time. And you can perhaps trick yourself a little further when you go back this last time to go over the manuscript.

Carry the box to your favorite spot on the couch or to the easy chair where you customarily read other stuff for pleasure. Relax. If you smoke, light up. If you drink, pour a weak one. Put your feet up, hum a tune. Have a tape recorder or pencil and pad handy, but not right on your lap.

Start reading your manuscript just as you would someone else's book. If you find a typographical error or something you want to fix, make a quick note onto the tape or notepad, but don't make a big deal of it, don't stop reading for longer than absolutely necessary, and don't get into the writer-editor configuration! You're a reader now!

Just try to read and enjoy.

You may find that it works amazingly well for a few pages, perhaps as many as thirty or forty. Then you'll find your attention flagging, or fatigue whispering more discouraging messages in your ear. At this point, put the manuscript aside for the night.

Pick it up again the next day in the same way. Having done this throughout the book, you may have a few things to fix up. Fix them.

And now you will have done more than 99 percent of the people who talk about writing ever do. You will have finished a novel. Congratulations! Any novel finished is better than all those masterworks that never get out of the talking stage. You have really done something and you should be proud of that. What now?

■■ SUBMITTING THE BOOK ■■

Writers' magazines are filled with articles about ways to place your manuscript. There are entire books on the subject. Some of the advice is good and some of it is nonsense. I'll make this section brief, pointing out a few basic hints that will help you avoid common pitfalls.

Don't bind or otherwise package your final manuscript. Loose pages, consecutively numbered, in a sturdy box, are preferred. Make copies of your work and keep them in separate locations. (I knew a writer once whose house burned, and both the original and the carbon of the manuscript, all that existed, were lost in the flames.)

If you can locate and obtain the services of a reputable New York literary agent, by all means do so.

There may be good literary agents working in places other than New York City, but I don't know of any. Agents on the West Coast tend to be movie-oriented, and the percentage of novels that sell to movies is tiny indeed. Most agents who work out of other parts of the country are, at best, informed mailing services and I would shun them. I've known writers who got royally screwed by some of them. A few give new meaning to the word "unscrupulous."

A few reputable agencies charge reading fees to new novelists; they make a sincere effort to sell the best work they re-
ceive, and charge back the reading fee against the advance
when the book sells. But far too many such agencies are con
operations that make their profits from reading fees and glow-
ing reader reports—then never sell a book. Shun these crooks.

Many top agents belong to a self-policing guild in New York.
They can be counted on to be ethical and honest. They have
separate royalty accounts for their writers, for example, so you
can be assured that the office secretary's salary won't come out
of your royalties before a check can be written for what's coming to you.

If you can't find a list of these agencies, and can't find a
publishing writer for some recommendations, write some
query letters to a dozen agencies listed in the Manhattan Yellow Pages. Briefly describe your novel and ask the agent if
she'll take a look. Await results and weigh your decision carefully.

If you've heard nothing in response to your query letter
after six weeks, you can assume the answer is "no."

Agents used to charge 10 percent as a commission. Many
now charge 15 percent. The extra 5 percent is often well worth
it in improved services. More than 15 percent, at this writing,
is unacceptable.

The publishing business is an insane asylum, and getting
worse by the day. Some agencies are taking on no new clients.
Few have time to tell you why they didn't like your book.
Don't ask and you won't be disappointed.

If you do get a letter suggesting changes, consider it most
carefully. This usually means the agent is definitely interested
in you. If you see the value of such suggestions, make the
changes and send the manuscript back to that agent again.

If you can't find an agent, there's no need to despair. Sometimes new authors find themselves in what looks like a Catch-
22 situation: to get a sale they need an agent, and to get an

agent they have to have made a sale. It ain't necessarily so. A few books are bought by publishers "over the transom."

So if you have to start submitting the novel on your own, write query letters to ten or fifteen publishers selected from *Writers' Market* or *Literary Market Place,* current copies of which ought to be in your bookstore or public library. If and when you get an okay, send a brisk, clean copy with a covering letter reminding the editor that she said you could send it, and then sit back to await developments. (Be sure to send along sufficient return postage.)

How long will you wait? Far too long. And getting longer. Three months is not unusual. After four, perhaps a discreet, short letter, asking how it's going, is in order. After six months, if all you've heard is silence, you can give up and ask to have the manuscript returned.

May you submit to more than one publisher at the same time? Sure. Do you tell them? Hell, no. What if you get two offers on the same book? You should be so lucky. Look for a star in the east. But if it happens, take the highest bid.

Once you have a prospective buyer for your book, incidentally, an agent is easier to find. Don't hesitate to recontact some of those agencies who may have rejected you earlier. Tell them, "I've sold my book and want you to represent me on contract." Chances are you'll find a taker now, and an agent earns her fee even when entering at this late stage; agencies generally can negotiate a better contract than you can.

There are a million questions new novelists have about selling the manuscript and about contracts. No book could anticipate all of them, and frankly I have no inclination even to try. If you duck the shyster agents and keep your manuscript in the mail to reputable publishers—not vanity houses that want to charge you money to publish—the book will eventually find a home. You have to believe that even in today's insane marketplace a good novel will be spotted and published. If you don't believe that, you'll go crazy.

Contract provisions are beyond the scope of this chapter. The Authors Guild offers a sample recommended contract. If and when you start selling, you'll want to join the guild, study the model contract, and try to get as many of its provisions into your contract as possible. Your agent will help with all of that.

Meanwhile, as all this is going on, you're of course at work on another novel, right? Because novelists write novels, right? So if the worst happens and you never sell this first book, by the time the bad news really sinks in you're going to have one or two more manuscripts in circulation as well.

There's a very old saying, about not putting all your eggs in one basket, that applies here, I think. As a novelist, you're a one-person fiction factory. Remember that. The one thing you can control is your continued work.

So work, already.

14

Final Words

Writers write,
and everyone else
talks about it.

At a time when the publishing business has never been crazier, and it's harder than ever to break in, what can be said at the end of a book designed for the aspiring novelist, or the writer aiming to improve his markets?

It was Goethe, I think, who said that the greatest thing in life is to have a goal and to be working diligently toward it. The world is full of people who make excuses for their failures to try. Wanting to write a good novel, and find readers for it, is a noble goal. Once you eschew excuses and steadfastly refuse to allow bitterness, you are embarked on a journey that will enrich your life and give you (at least) a ticket in a lottery far richer than any state government offers.

The period 1957–60 or so was a bad time in publishing. I've

been told that no one broke in during that time. Luckily, I heard this only after I had sold my first novel in 1957, and six more in the next two years. So my own experience contradicts the naysayers. And you can, too.

If you write a good enough book, it will sell. And if this one isn't good enough, if you keep analyzing and working and growing and writing, the next one, or the one after that, *will* be good enough.

And that one will sell.

We have to believe that, all of us. We're in an international competition, you and I, and only the best will survive. But we can never be beaten unless we give up.

Let us, then, work to become the best that we can be, and have faith that everything else we dream about will follow.

Good luck!

Bibliography

Bellow, Saul. *Herzog*. New York: Viking, 1964.

Berne, Eric. *Games People Play*. New York: Grove Press, 1964.

Bickham, Jack M. *Katie, Kelly and Heck*. New York: Doubleday, 1973.

Campbell, Walter S. *Writing: Advice and Devices*. New York: Doubleday, 1950.

Clinton, Jeff. *The Fighting Buckaroo*. New York: Berkley Medallion, 1961.

Edmonds, J. M., ed. *The Characters of Theophrastus*. Cambridge: Harvard University Press, 1946.

Fast, Julius. *Body Language*. New York: Pocket Books, 1971.

Fleming, Ian. *Goldfinger*. New York: Macmillan, 1959.

Foster-Harris, William. *The Basic Formulas of Fiction*. Norman: University of Oklahoma Press, 1944.

Hayakawa, S. I. *Symbol, Status and Personality*. New York: Harcourt, Brace & World, 1963.

Herrigel, Eugen. *Zen in the Art of Archery*. New York: Vintage Books, 1971.

Hills, Rust. "Fiction." *Esquire*, October 1973.

Hoffer, Eric. *The Ordeal of Change*. New York: Harper Colophon, 1964.

Karpman, S. "Fairy Tales and Script Drama Analysis." *Transactional Analysis Bulletin*, Spring, 1968.

Lynn, Mary, and Georgia McKinney. *Every Page Perfect*. Albuquerque: CompuPress, Inc., 1987.

MacDonald, John D. *Darker Than Amber*. New York: Gold Medal, 1966.

Steere, David A. *Bodily Expressions in Psychotherapy*. New York: Bruner/Mazel, 1982.

Steiner, Claude M. *Scripts People Live*. New York: Grove Press, 1974.

Swain, Dwight V. *Techniques of the Selling Writer*. Norman: University of Oklahoma Press, 1958.

Thrall, William Flint, and Addison Hibbard. *A Handbook to Literature*. New York: Odyssey Press, 1936.

Wellek, Rene, and Austin Warren. *Theory of Literature*. New York: Harcourt, Brace, 1949.

Whitney, Phyllis A. *The Trembling Hills*. New York: Fawcett Crest, 1965.

Wouk, Herman. *The Caine Mutiny*. New York: Doubleday, 1951.

Index